BUTLER OF WANTAGE

WILLIAM JOHN BUTLER
1846

BUTLER OF WANTAGE

His Inheritance and his Legacy

An offering from his Community of

S. MARY THE VIRGIN

dacre press
westminster

PRINTED IN GREAT BRITAIN BY ROBERT MACLEHOSE AND CO. LTD.
THE UNIVERSITY PRESS, GLASGOW

IN PACE DEI REQUIESCAT
PASTOR ANIMARUM
SAGAX SIMPLEX STRENUUS
WILLELMUS JOHANNES BUTLER S.T.P.
QUI NATUM SE ATQUE RENATUM
NON SIBI SED CHRISTO OVIBUSQUE CHRISTI RATUS
AUSTERA QUADAM CARITATE
LABORE INDEFESSO ASSIDUA PRECE
ID EGIT
DOMI FORIS VALIDUS AEGROTANS
UT AMOREM DEI ERGA PECCATORES TESTATUS
A PECCATIS REDUCES IN AMORE DEI CONFIRMARET [1]

Shepherd of souls, wise, simple, strong,
deeming himself both born and born again,
not for himself, but for Christ and for Christ's sheep—
With love that could be stern, with toil unwearied
and with ceaseless prayer, he wrought to this effect,
in private and in public, sick and well,
that showing forth the love of God to sinners,
he strengthened in the love of God the souls
brought back from sin.

[1] Memorial inscription in Lincoln Cathedral (translated by
:SMV.) on alabaster altar tomb.

ACKNOWLEDGMENT

OUR thanks are due to Messrs. Macmillan & Co. Ltd. for the use of quotations from the *Life and Letters of Dean Butler*, and to Messrs. Methuen & Co. Ltd. for references to an essay on 'Bishop Butler' by Dr. Spooner in a series of *Leaders of Religion*, both long out of print.

We are also indebted to *Wantage Past and Present* published in 1901, for local historical details. And to Messrs. Geoffrey Bles Ltd. for the use of a quotation from the words of Charles, Lord Halifax, regarding Mrs. Butler, in Chapter 4 of Part II.

CONTENTS

PART ONE

THE INHERITANCE

PART TWO

THE HEIR

PART THREE

HIS LEGACY

ILLUSTRATIONS

PART ONE
THE INHERITANCE

THE INHERITANCE

The little town of Wantage, lying at the foot of the Berkshire downs, might seem to have been left completely aside by the tide of life, for it has no main coach road and is not an obvious highway from one important place to another; it is nearly three miles from the nearest station—and even that came as an afterthought some years after the line was completed. Wantage had as little use for an intrusive railway as the world seems to have had for Wantage. Yet Wantage has made a great and notable contribution to the very foundations of national life, for it was there that Alfred the Great was born. Though the actual site of his birthplace is uncertain, tradition has it that he was born at a place where three streams meet; and we may truly think of these as figuring the stream of English national life, the stream of English religious life and the stream of English education which, when joined together, were to fertilize and irrigate in an ever increasing tide. If therefore we attempt to trace the three streams to their source it will not be merely an antiquarian prelude but rather the recognition of an influence that has never ceased but which, like the springs that issue from the high chalkland of the downs, may disappear for awhile underground only to re-appear again in unexpected places and at unexpected times.

Alfred, born in 848 or 849, was the son of Ethelwulf, King of the West Saxons, and Osburh his wife, and though the youngest of three sons was, according to Asser, Bishop of Sherborne, his friend and biographer, 'loved by his father and mother and even by all the people, above all his brothers'—a very Benjamin. Pleasant rising ground to the west of Wantage Church may well mark the site where Ethelwulf's timbered hall once stood. The highest point was known as Limburh[1] (i.e. adjacent to the Burh) and here Roman potsherds and coins and two wells have been found; to the south the land slopes gently to 'the Ham', a property in a well watered valley that marks the site of an early settlement—the name could mean no less. Between the two stands the Mead, once known as King's Mead, an ancient name and a fertile site over-looking the present town, with a stream below that is actually fed by three streams, one of which has been always known as Alfred's spring and well,[2] the waters of which are accounted to have medicinal qualities. Below in an old hollow road leading to a ford stands Willoughby's Mill, bought by the family of the present owner[3] in 1596 from the Dean and Canons of Windsor[4] and still busily working. This mill is one of the four mentioned in Domesday Book; it is here that the waters meet, the

[1] The site of the Convent of St. Mary the Virgin and now spelled Limborough.

[2] Alfred's spring was, by a coincidence, used for adult baptisms by a baptist named Alfred Hazell in the last century, but the name is none the less of ancient origin.

[3] Mr. Willoughby, the owner of the Mill, died in 1944.

[4] The royal demesne of Wantage was alienated from the crown by Richard I (1189–1199) who gave or sold it to the Earl of Albemarle. The estate was held by the Earl till 1190; it passed into the pos-session of Fulk FitzWaryn in 1215. Six or seven Fulks succeeded one another until we find an Ivo FitzWaryn in the fifteenth century as lord of the manor of 'Wanting Brian'; he was the father-in-law of the celebrated Dick Whittington. Part, however, of the royal property had already passed to the possession of a priory of Benedictine monks, a cell of the Abbey of Ogburn, Wilts, but in close connection with the parent Abbey of Bec Herlouin in Normandy, to whom the town of Wantage was paying a tallage in 1247. The Priory may date from the reign of Henry II (1254–1189) as it was he who presented the advowson to the Abbey of Bec. The Priory was dissolved with all

spring from the Ark, a former mill higher up on the Downs, the Letcombe brook and Alfred's spring. Not many yards away is the Icknield or Ickleton Way[1] dividing the Ham from the Mead and Limborough, while Gallows Lane nearby seems to suggest sinister manorial rights. If this is the locality in which 'England's Darling' first saw the light, first looked on the English countryside, there could be no more characteristic or intimate view.

Two journeys took Alfred when still a little boy to Rome, the first when he was only five years old, an early exile from his home and from the mother whom he was never to see again; the second a few years later when he may have travelled back with his young step-mother, Judith, the thirteen-year-old daughter of Charles the Bald. On his first visit he was received as 'Bishop's son' by Pope Leo IV, a probable allusion to his confirmation, while then, or later, he was invested with the crown, and purple and white mantle of consular rank—which honour many held to be a forecast of his coming kingship.

These early travels meant also an early entrance into a world of culture and learning that his eager child mind readily absorbed. He must have attended one of the Scholae attached to the Roman Basilicas, if not the Saxon School itself on the Vatican Hill; but that had been but lately destroyed by fire and was to be rebuilt, it is said, by his father. 'Romeburh', as Alfred afterwards wrote, would in any case have extended his education in chant and song, studies always dear to him, and have given him a

other alien monasteries by Henry V, 'for taking part with the French against the King of England', and the advowson and at least part of the land was transferred to the Dean and Canons of Windsor. Thus the Dean and Canons of Windsor were able to write in 1639 in defence of their title deeds: 'From the Crowne they come to us entire, by the Kings Charter.'

[1] The way of the Iceni.

first introduction to those Christian Classics that he was afterwards to translate into Anglo-Saxon for his people, adding his own shrewd notes and comments that so closely interpret his own and the English mind.

The boy may have been at his father's second marriage and have seen something of the splendour of the West Frankish Court, and Judith would certainly have taught him more of that wider world about which Orosius had written in his History, another book that Alfred was to put into Anglo-Saxon. We cannot think of these children in terms of years, they were so quickly mature, learned in so many tongues, aware of world happenings, proficient in sport and arms. Life was strenuous and full of danger; it blossomed early and was quickly past, so that if it were not grasped at once there could be no recall. Alfred's three elder brothers died in early manhood, and he was himself subject to some recurrent complaint which conflicted throughout his life with all his eager, far-sighted schemes.[1] In every way time pressed.

The cares of sovereignty fell upon him when he was only twenty-three, and it was a harassed realm, overrun by invaders, that he was called upon to rule. By 878 Alfred had known all the bitterness of defeat and humiliation at the hands of the Danes; now came the turning point in his fortunes and his great victory in the battle of Ethandun[2] even though it was won at the expense of ceding the half of England to the invader, set him free at length to work out his true vocation as the father of the English tradition and of English education. Contented with his little

[1] This might have been epilepsy, stone (he suffered great pain) or asthma.

[2] Ethandun is located at Eddington, Wilts., near the White Horse on Bratton Hill; but it is curious that in Alfred's will he associated Ethandun with Wantage and Lambourn in his legacy to his wife, the latter places being but a short distance apart.

kingdom, 'Alfred the Truthteller' never dreamed of a Great or Greater Britain, but he saw clearly and steadily the only foundations on which a State can be built, the only bond by which a people can be united; his strong foundations were capable of sustaining unlimited extension.

It would be ridiculous to suggest that he foresaw the future or visualised democratic freedom, but just as the springs of his birthplace join and find their way into the Thames, so his love for and understanding of his people, his 'insatiable desire for knowledge' (to quote Asser), and his strong religious convictions were bound to find their way into the ever flowing waters of a full national life. Alfred's legal code, his royal 'doombook', is based on the Decalogue and stands for righteousness; his education was to be widespread: 'let all the free born youth now in England who are able be set to learn, so long as they are unfit for other occupations, until they can read well the English script. Let those afterwards be taught the Latin tongue who are to be educated further, and raised to higher estate.'[1] He established a school for nobles in connection with his palace and minster at Winchester, the precursor of Wykeham's Foundation and of all public schools, and there his two elder sons were taught, while Edward and Æthelthryth, the younger children, were educated within the palace yet sharing the same curriculum. There was to be neither rich nor poor, male nor female in Alfred's plans for education, and as time passed his translations dispersed learning throughout the kingdom, finding their way into many homes. More than this, they brought the people into touch with the King's mind and outlook both by preface and comment. Two main streams, that of English tradition and English education were rising; there remained that third stream of English religion that was to add its healing properties to the other two.

[1] Alfred's preface to St. Gregory's Pastoralia.

Alfred's religious devotion showed itself early, but may have suffered some eclipse in adolescence, as he considered that his defeat at the hands of the Danes was due to his former neglect of the poor. Asser records 'his fixed purpose of holy meditation', probably part of that 'service of body and mind that he devoted to God even to the half of his time', and his scrupulous rules for the disposal of his money. Two books were always with him, a book of Psalms and Prayers that he 'carried in his bosom' and an anthology of quotations made at Asser's suggestion, his *Enchiridion* or Manual, 'flower blossomings' from many gardens. The king was a devoted son of the Church, providing funds for churches and religious foundations all over England and 'as far as Ireland' and making his own special foundations for monks at Athelney and for nuns at Shaftesbury—where his second daughter, Aethelgyth, was Abbess.

In this regard a clause in his will carries a special interest to Wantage, a special link with subsequent Wantage history. The clause is obscure, it runs:

'I will that the people of Domrahamme are given their landbook and their freedom to choose as they please. For me and for Aelflede[1] and for the friends that she prayed for and that I pray for—and let each one seek also my soul's health by deathless contract. So be it and as it is fitting and as you wish me to be forgiven.'

And this may be rendered thus:

'I will to the ladies of the Domrahamme (fem. genitive plural of *Dominae* in Saxonized Latin) are given their title deeds and their freedom to choose as they please (a fourteenth century translation runs: "on which hand or direction they please"). For me and for Aelflede[1] and

---

[1] Aelflede, Alfred's eldest daughter, married Aethelred Ealdorman of Mercia, was known as the Lady of the Mercians and became justly famous.

for the friends that she prayed for and that I pray for. And let each one seek also the good of my soul by perpetual intercession (the word also signifies obligation). So be it and as it is fitting and as you wish me to be forgiven.'

In the fourteenth century translation there is added: 'and the needy that be living,' and one Latin translation adds: 'Pro vivorum ac defunctorum.'

Despite obscurities it would appear that the Domrahamme[1] was a community concerned with intercession; and this corresponds to the 'alien priory of black nuns' mentioned by Dugdale in the Monasticon as being established before the Conquest at 'Hamme in Barkshire'. Speed, Leland and Tanner speak of this Convent as being 'as early as the reign of King John', but Dugdale says it was closed before the Conquest, though it was possibly revived in the reign of John (1199–1216). It may therefore be suggested that the tunschip or stockade enclosure surrounding Limburh, King's Mead and the Ham included this alien community, which had possibly been founded by Ethelwulf for foreign nuns for, as Alfred was to find later, 'the love of the monastic life had utterly decayed from the (English) nation.' The site has all the amenities of meadow, streams and mill[2] necessary to the needs of a community and the house may well have played some part in Alfred's childhood and that of his own children. The present convent of St. Mary the Virgin on the higher ground of Limborough would be separated in space only by meadow and trees from the home of the early nuns in the valley, though in space of time at least 1,000 years passed between the two foundations.

Here then is a great inheritance, great and far-reaching influences gathered round the birthplace of a king. In his preface and notes to the Pastoralia and the Soliloquies

[1] Compare with Nunnaminster, Winchester.
[2] Mentioned in Domesday Book as one of the four mills.

Alfred plays with two illustrations, both of which are apposite. In the Pastoralia he speaks of St. Gregory's wisdom as 'the waters which the God of Hosts promised as a comfort to us earthdwellers', and he pictures water meadows, as at the Ham, or water falling into a well like that which may have been in his own home enclosure. He speaks also of men as pitchers, sound or broken, designed to carry the water out to the needy world. In the Soliloquies he writes of his work of translation as that of a man gathering wood from a forest for the building of his house and adds 'I exhort everyone who is able and has many wains to wend his way to the same wood'.

In Wantage and in different ways and various centuries men have, like Alfred's pitchers, carried the same waters for the service of their Church and country, they have gathered their materials for building from many periods and countries and often, quite unconsciously, from the king himself.

PART TWO

THE HEIR

Chapter One

THE SPRING OF EDUCATION

So far the inheritance—the newly appointed vicar of Wantage, William John Butler, who arrived in 1847 with his tightly-buttoned frock coat, white stock and high hat, hardly looked like the heir of the ages. He was only twenty-nine, he was grave and solemn for his years and saw his future parish in terms of souls who were in spiritual peril. His was a really beautiful face notwithstanding its gravity, yet one that in the course of years and work was to become a little severe, with firm lips and piercing eyes. It was fortunate that he could already depend on courage and determination, for the first congregation recorded in his diary numbered only thirty-five, and his parish account but lately opened at the bank amounted to ten pounds. His immediate inheritance might have been a cause for despondency, for his predecessor had not attempted to live in the dilapidated vicarage but had chosen to reside genteelly at Oxford a full twelve miles away. The lethargy that had fallen upon the church in the eighteenth century and had continued on into the nineteenth century still lay upon Wantage like a pall; and lethargy hates to be aroused. It would be difficult to over-estimate the loss in English tradition caused by the Hanoverian succession. Convocation had been suppressed from a nervous political anxiety that the Church might side with the Stuarts; bishops were appointed for political reliability rather than for any spiritual qualifications; enthusiasm was deliberately barred; evangelisation had almost ceased to exist; a vague deism from the Continent represented the fashionable religion. Every effort to arouse life and ardour was shouted down with the cry of 'no popery'; even Wesley had not been exempt and the Lord George Gordon riots had gone far to set the city ablaze. The Tractarians in their turn were exposed to the same abuse, and at the time when faith and morals had fallen to a very low ebb, the Church seemed unable to make any vital contribution to national life.

Wantage as described in 1847 had a bad name as a well-known refuge for runaway criminals, who found the downs convenient as hiding places from the law; it was for this reason that it was known as 'Black Wantage'.[1] Serious crimes had been recently committed: there had been a murder at the Packhorse Inn, there was rough bull baiting at the Camel and, as there were no less than twelve public houses additional to those now in existence and private brewing was common, drunkenness and brawling were widespread. At that time the principal trades of the town were brewing and malting.

Men still wore smock frocks and low-crowned beaver hats and women red cloaks with pattens for muddy days, the little town had not as yet crept out along the Charlton Road, and for the moment life seemed static, changing but little in the full hundred years. There were practically no spiritual influences to stimulate to new endeavour, or to counteract the downward trend of life—except perhaps that of the Baptists, who were in possession of the Mead and had converted Alfred's spring and well into a 'bath' for their baptisms, lining it with brick for the purpose. It was said that Bunyan had preached in the original Baptist chapel in the seventeenth century; some Baptists had certainly suffered for their faith in 1642 and had had to retire to Grove nearby, there to continue their devotions in private.

[1] After Butler's death an obituary notice drew attention to the fact 'that by nature he was devoted to family life, humorous and full of gentle kindness but was austere by reason of his flaming desire to expunge the blackness of sin from "Black Wantage" and elsewhere.'

The railway had been opened in 1840, a train at that time taking eight hours from London to Bristol, but the station for Wantage was at Challow, 3 miles off, whither a bus went twice a day; coal and agricultural produce were carried by the Wilts and Berks canal. Night-watchmen still cried the hours up to 1856, and there was no one who was responsible for order. Oil lamps gave their feeble light till 1874, and there were no macadamised roads until the same date.

William John Butler faced his uphill task with a determination directed towards two main lines of advance—the restoration of Church life and worship and the provision of education, but like Bishop Blomfield of London he was bold enough to give education precedence and postponed any attempt at the restoration of the parish church until the National Schools were begun in 1849; for, as he writes in his diary, 'they are to me the great object on which we expend all strength.' He realised from the first that 'the battle of the Church must be won in the schools' and he made Hosea's words, 'my people perish for lack of knowledge,' the inspiration of his life.

Neither did he 'draw the line' or exclude anyone, not even the outcast, for, turning his attention to the Workhouse set on the steep hill rising to the Ridgeway on the Downs, the young vicar was confronted with the heterogeneous crowd of needy and vagrant folk that gathered under the Poor Law in the middle of the last century. They represented a new and almost insoluble problem, and he wrote in his diary: 'The mixture of characters in the Union is one of the greatest evils, it requires the attention of a resident Chaplain;' and yet, after catechising the children there, he was so touched by their response that he wrote: 'It is nothing but the clumsiness and the bad arrangements of a heathen Poor Law which can prevent them growing up in love and faith; and as the one is an accident and the other the permanent grace of God, may we not hope that, at length, the power and opportunity may be permitted to His Church to deal thoroughly with these his little ones and give them a real christian education. There is the ground, if only we might till it.'

In this spirit he set to work to raise money to build church schools and made the bold venture of launching two simultaneous schemes, the one for the national schools, the other to refound and develop the old Latin school that had its home in what might well have been King Alfred's ancient church. 'Church Education was a subject very near my father's heart', his younger daughter Mary wrote shortly before her death in 1937, 'and he used to say "faith, grind and prayer will win all things".' It certainly needed all three to win through, but the young vicar, bringing his plans to a successful conclusion, saw the foundation stone of the new King Alfred Grammar School laid on the same day as the opening of his new national schools. It was a great occasion. The Bishop of Oxford (Samuel Wilberforce), Archdeacon Manning and Doctor Pusey walked in the procession while the choir sang *Angulare Fundamentum*, one of Butler's favourite hymns, a thousand people being present. Although vandalism destroyed the old Latin School in 1851, many of its ancient features had been so entirely lost that it was described in the end as mainly 'Elizabethan'; but Butler saved the Norman doorway and various fragments from the canopy of a tomb, building them into King Alfred's School; it was at least some effort to emphasise continuity.

Mary Butler remembered that in those early days the curates, (and her father always had an eminent staff), were expected to be present when he was teaching in school, but were only allowed themselves to hear each child repeat its morning and evening prayer. One or other of them painted a series of frescoes in the top schoolroom: art as well as education were to be made available for the people.

Butler next turned his attention to the higher education of girls by founding what was then called a Middle School, first housed in the quaint old Back Street room approached by steps. Growing rapidly, the school soon had to move to two houses in Newbury Street and became known as St. Katharine's, but the vicar did not live to see its final home in the large school built on the FitzWaryn Manor of 'Wanting Brian', although he must have planned this before his death. A further house, used originally as a home for girls, was re-opened in 1873 as St. Mary's School for Girls, corresponding in many ways to all that Miss Beale and Miss Buss were doing for women's education in Cheltenham and London at about the same time. So successful was St. Mary's from its inception that in the recollection of one of the first pupils (now aged eighty-four) the Vicar said 'he would never be content until he had twelve St. Mary's Schools in England'.

It would have been little use to develop schools without a corresponding effort to develop teachers, so that from the first, in 1850, Butler began a small training centre which eventually occupied buildings known as St. Michael's, situated on the site of the Benedictine Priors' Hold. The property had been left to him by Mrs. Trevelyan, and many recollections gather round that house and the cottages in Newbury Street where this work first started. It is not surprising that Butler had said in the midst of his early struggles and in the days of grind that 'one more school would kill me', but the training at St. Michael's was always a pure delight to him. In recent years the Guild of the Good Shepherd, that grew out of his work but was known to him only as a small tentative group, has extended even beyond Great Britain, having 1,334 members, of whom 116 are African, Chinese or Indian

Christians. Out of the Guild again, the Third Order of Jesus the Good Shepherd has lately been approved by authority and includes primary and secondary teachers, many still teaching in State schools but living under rule, with their own central house and several of their own recognised schools. Even in early days one of the Government Inspectors had said that he had known many teachers trained at Wantage but had never come across a failure. No wonder that Bishop Wilberforce, recalling a visit to the parish, wrote: 'at Wantage there was no rest day or night. Everything was done with full activity by day and, at night, first there were conversations lasting into the small hours and then the doves cooed and the clock chimed.' Bishop Stubbs was to comment later that 'Butler's work is amazing'.

When in 1880 Butler was appointed to a Canonry at Worcester his passion for education set him to work once again and he founded a Girls' High School, claiming Miss Alice Ottley, against her will, to become headmistress with the conclusive words 'it is a call and you must come'. This school was also to meet with success, and in Worcester it was said of him that 'verily had his path laid in that direction he would have been the greatest Headmaster of the century'. In 1891 he dwelt on the worthlessness of any education, religious or secular, which had not for its foundation the careful teaching of dogma: and showed clearly that it was only from a knowledge of the right Faith that any intelligible reason for a right Practice could be drawn.

First interviews with Butler were not a little alarming; one of his students describes 'a tall figure, balanced on the arm of a Windsor chair with an eyeglass stuck in one eye—those wonderfully keen blue eyes'. Another speaking of her admission to a Guild remembered that 'he took my hand and admitted me, his eyes looked me through and through until he saw right out on the other side'.

Even a girl clearing a refectory table who was sorely tempted to steal sugar told one of the Sisters 'how could I take the sugar while he was looking at me like that'—and she was only alone with his photograph. Bishop King of Lincoln, however, recalled the words of a little child—and children were never afraid of him—who could not keep back her tears when she heard that he had died 'because he was so kind and nice'. There were certainly two sides to his strong character.

There was no fear or restraint when the Vicar took the St. Michael's students for long walks over the downs or on expeditions as far as Oxford, Dorchester, Fairford or Wayland's Smithy; Charlotte Yonge, a great personal friend, was often a member of these parties. As they walked he would tell them thrilling stories of the neighbourhood and say that 'nothing is more stirring than the lives of men who have nobly served our Lord—they help one to long and try'. It may be that Alfred was in his mind. He loved to startle and stimulate by asking unexpected questions or making puzzling statements: 'It is the hardest thing in the world,' he would say, 'to make people think.' The girls answered wildly at times, trying to keep up with his rapid thought, and one answer amused him so much that he said 'he should laugh if he remembered it on the sickest of sick beds'. He had 'a funny way of asking a question in mental arithmetic' without any warning, and when he asked 'how many rules there were in arithmetic his answer was always one, the rule of common-sense'.[1]

[1] These violent and unexpected questions were not unlike the methods of Bishop Butler, a Wantage man of the seventeenth century. Tucker his contemporary biographer, relates that when walking with the Bishop he suddenly stopped and asked 'what security is there against the insanity of individuals? The physicians know of none'; and then, after a pause, 'why may not whole communities be seized with insanity as well as individuals?' A pertinent question for 1939–47.

Many stories gather round his work and play with these young students, and they had to be always prepared for the unexpected. When still living in the Newbury Street cottages in 1849, they recall, he would appear at their door before 6 a.m. suspecting that the rising bell was not being rung punctually and ring it vigorously himself. On one occasion he called from beneath the window to ask if they were up and, when a shamed voice confessed that they were not, he called back cheerfully 'Dry bread for breakfast and be in my study at 8 a.m.'. If they were punctual 'he would order hot rolls for their breakfast from the baker's shop next door, and sometimes eggs'. One former student remembers how a French lesson was suddenly interrupted when he looked through an open window to call out 'That pronunciation is very bad, I will come and take the lesson myself'. Indeed the Vicar taught on almost any subject and on Saturdays they had to show examination papers of which no detail was left unobserved. The music teachers used to take very good places in the diocesan examinations, and sometimes a St. Michael's student stood first on the list. Commenting on two teachers in a small church school he said 'One is too much Mary and the other too much Martha, so perhaps between them they may accomplish something'.

As Butler's educational and training work became known Wantage gained a wide reputation. He 'educated for character', which meant the enrichment and strengthening of personality, and was always convinced that 'true education consists in giving up present pleasures for future gains'. It is good to be known as 'a character' and certainly the term describes the then Vicar of Wantage, and he, in his turn, welcomed anyone, even those who opposed him, who spoke their mind and showed grit. Once a teacher refused to go and tidy a classroom that had been left in disorder, saying quietly 'I have been engaged to teach children and not to tidy rooms'. Butler looked her up and down and said, ' Well, there's some stuff in you.' Short words of praise often followed such a blunt answer, such as, 'She'll do,' 'She's no goose,' 'She's got some fun in her.' Once he was interviewing a teacher, 'standing on the hearthrug with his back to the fire and his keen eyes taking one in from head to foot:' the questions that he asked were puzzling, concerned with her family, her father and his work, her brothers in the Civil Service and Engineers, but he ended 'with a humorous twinkle in his eyes, "Ah! I see you've got brains in your family".' When about to hand over a part of his work to Father Maxwell, S.S.J.E., then a Curate of the Parish, the latter declared he would never be able to manage the children, but Butler reassured him by saying that he had himself thrown a book at a girl—'but', he added meditatively, 'I took good care to miss her.' It is difficult to exaggerate the stormy, zealous, energising character of the man, or the strong contrasts in his character.

There are short notes in his diary for the confirmation classes in 1850. It is a grave syllabus with no touch of emotion or rhetoric, following closely on the Ignatian method on which almost all the Retreats of that period were based, as notes possessed by the community of St. Mary the Virgin prove. The course he marked out runs as follows: 'The creation of Adam. His probation, fall and punishment. Change of nature from innocent to sinful. Effect of the change, cf. Romans 1. Need of a new nature. Promise in the beginning. Coming of Christ. We must be united with and grafted into Christ, that changes our nature from sin to grace. How are we to be grafted? God works by means. (Tree of Life, Jericho, Naaman, Five thousand fed.) Nature of Sacraments. Baptism. Baptismal vow. How are we to keep it? God gives grace. How? Holy Communion, Confirmation. Read the service.

Give final directions. Invite to Holy Communion.' It is a stiff syllabus and was taught with serious urgency, but it worked; the candidates did not forget, as notebooks carefully written out and treasured still show.

No practical detail of behaviour escaped his observation and many were embodied in rules given to the children whom he taught; there was to be 'the strict observance of silence before Communion, including no turning over of leaves, no use of handkerchiefs, no coughs: this silence to be maintained until after their thanksgiving; not to pray leaning on elbows nor to cover the face with hands during responses: to say "Amen" clearly: to follow the lessons in the Bible: to keep silence walking to and from church.' They were taught to observe great courtesy, such as rising when spoken to by a Sister or Mistress, opening the door for a Mistress, good manners to all especially 'to any whom we might deem inferior to ourselves', punctuality and attention to bells, 'getting out of bed the minute the bell rang, etc.'

We have spoken of the inheritance associated with Alfred the Great and the three streams of his birthplace. It is not fanciful to believe that the King would have found a congenial mind in the young Victorian in the tightly-buttoned frock coat, with his 'insatiable desire for knowledge'.[1] One stream at least, the stream of education, had been set free in Wantage and, gathering strength through the years, was to find its way as far as India and South Africa—thus extending the education of girls in Christian faith and sound learning even beyond William John Butler's wildest dreams. Faith, grind and prayer had accomplished much.

[1] Asser.

BETTER OF WANTAGE

Chapter II

THE SPRING OF SPIRITUAL LIFE

Two religious foundations were associated with Wantage in the past, as we have seen, the Domrahamme
of Alfred's will and the Benedictine Priory, established
during the reign of Henry II, on royal property which has
been known to this day as Priors Hold; both were alien
houses, owing to the infrequency of religious vocation in
England at that time. The Benedictine monks were from
Normandy, a cell from the Abbey of S. Mary at Bec; and
it is likely that the ruins of the second foundation in the
reign of King John were also Norman. Bec was famed for
its regularity and learning, for which Henry I, Stephen and
Henry II showed special approval; an abbey that had
already given Lanfranc (†1089) and Anselm (†1109) to
England as Archbishops of Canterbury, to be followed in
1138 by Theobald also. When the FitzWaryns became
possessed of the royal manor of Wantage and with that of
'Wanting Bryan' at the further end of the town, they
brought with them something of the magnificence and
solidarity of Norman culture and gave to Wantage its fine
transitional church. Wantage Church, dedicated to St.
Peter and St. Paul, certainly represents the assertive
strength and dogmatic order of the period; the massive
pillars of the lantern would suffice to show that. Nowadays,
with encroaching houses and garden walls, the large
cruciform building seems to crouch upon its site like some
heraldic creature ready to spring, but in earlier days it
would have dominated the higher ground that rises from
Letcombe brook, then already joined by the two other
streams. Within the churchyard there once stood a far

more ancient church that had doubtless proved too small
and insignificant for the growing town—a Saxon church
built it may have been by Ethelwulf, the place, perhaps
of Alfred's baptism. Part of an eighth century preaching
cross was found in the churchyard and is preserved in the
present church. This chapel, for such it must have been,
was roughly handled by time, as in 1351 it was already so
seriously out of repair that a special indulgence was
granted to any who prayed there on the five Feasts of our
Lady, a spiritual privilege that was frankly to be applied
to its restoration. In Elizabeth's reign this chapel was
altered, it is likely out of all recognition, for use as the first
Grammar School, so that Wantage boys may well claim
their kinship with Alfred. The remains of this historic
building were finally swept away, as we have seen, in 1851.

Sir Ivo FitzWaryn in the fifteenth century added a
chantry chapel at the eastern end 'to the honour of the
Blessed Virgin and all Saints', that prayer might be made
for the repose of the souls of his father and mother, himself
and his heirs, 'wherein *placebo* and *dirige* with the new
lection and lauds following, *scilicit*' were to be sung on
the vigil of Sts. Simon and Jude. His will also contains
the bequest of his 'best furred gown' to his sister Philippe,
a nun of Wilton. They were evidently sons of the Church
who would have found the monks of Priors Hold congenial
neighbours and for whom, indeed, the long and gracious
choir of the parish church was built. According to their
generation and opportunity they also carried the waters
of education and of the spiritual life like the good pitchers
of Alfred's illustration to the men and women of a newer
age. In their holding, the stream of the English tradition
was enriched by continental experience—for it has ever
been part of the best English development to receive, use
and assimilate codes, customs and experience from lands
other than our own, while the moments of complete

insularity have always marked a period of ignorance and slothfulness in thought and life.

Both religious houses were suppressed on account of the French wars in the fifteenth century, when patriotic fervour overrode Catholicity and religious vocations were once again at a low ebb, no fresh house being founded in or near Wantage for the next four hundred years. Yet it is curious to note that the call of God to live the dedicated life is seldom unheard for long[1] and that it comes to men and women in the most unexpected places and periods and under the strangest conditions—as in the Civil War of the seventeenth century or the subsequent restoration. Many vocations can be traced, and women at least were living 'the recluse life' alone or in twos and threes in those uneasy centuries. Therefore less than a hundred years after William Law had died[2] the leaders of the Oxford Movement were already petitioning the Bishop of London to set free the springs of the religious life in England once again.

In 1845 William John Butler was staying with an old friend in Devonshire and, seemingly by chance, had much talk on religious vocation with the pretty and vivacious daughter of the house. He found in her a kindred spirit,

---

[1] Dr. Spence Jones in *The Golden Age of the Church* notes 'a strange power of recovery, after constantly recurring periods of fading away in spirit and in life . . . this power of recovery is one of the most remarkable features of the institution ', i.e. that of monasticism.

[2] Law had lived an almost monastic life at Kingscliffe, Northants., with his two friends, Mrs. Hutchinson and Hester Gibbon; their rule centred round the recitation of the Day Hours and their zeal for works of mercy to relieve the poor was such that the village had to beg them to desist, as their almsgiving collected a throng of undesirable beggars. Law also provided a library for the village, one of the first public libraries to exist, and this gives some indication of the capacity for thought and appreciation among an imperfectly educated people. The published catalogue is interesting and illuminating.

eager to dedicate herself to the service of God, one who, notwithstanding strong and sustained parental opposition, was to find her heart's desire in the community he was to found, there to become, in due time, a much beloved novice mistress, while no less than four of her nieces were to follow her example. A stream does not seem to lose force though it be hidden for a while. By 1847 Butler had already made his plan for the foundation of a 'Sisterhood' to act as the handmaids of the Church in the education of the young and in constant active service among the sick and poor. He had even decided to train Sisters to go out as teachers to neighbouring villages two by two, an idea that he probably adapted from the work of the French *Regent.* founded by Nicholas Pavillon, Bishop of Alet, in the seventeenth century. He knew of one if not more 'vocations in hiding', women who were only awaiting a clear call. Others of his Oxford neighbours were working along the same lines. In 1841 Marion Rebecca Hughes had made profession of vows in Oxford, but had very wisely postponed any attempt to form a community until she had spent some months in the study of the religious life mainly that of the Ursuline rule, in France, and had gained practical experience as a worker in the parish of her cousin, Canon Chamberlain, St. Thomas the Martyr, Oxford. Her society of the Holy and Undivided Trinity came into being in 1849. Dr. Pusey had also started a little group of mission sisters in Park Village, Regent's Park, as early a 1845.

It was in 1848 that the young vicar of Wantage boldly gathered together three or four women with the view to their forming a community under the leadership of Elizabeth Crawford Lockhart. Miss Lockhart was a gifted young woman, cultured and well born, who appeared to be the ideal leader: Butler's dream was beginning to take shape, but it was none the less a bold beginning in those days of prejudice. A small cottage in Wallingford Street, Wantage, was chosen, and it was there that Elizabeth and her few companions first began to live the common life and to recite the daily office from the Sarum Day Hours, which had been translated in 1845 by Albany Christie. These small books, containing the daily offices for a week, were carefully printed in special type with red rubrics, and bound attractively enough in parchment. This pleasant little touch of art and even elegance would seem to mark the youth and aspirations of the eager group. Butler, writing about this time to Keble, said 'Though you probably know them better than I do, I would mention the Hours translated by Albany Christie. I have found, as I think, great advantage for myself in using the Latin Hours and I cannot imagine anything that would take their place. The Sisters of St. Mary's Home use the Hours in English. Our bishop (Wilberforce) I *believe* saw them and made no objection. Indeed why should he? There is, as you know, very little to alter for the simple reason that they are Catholic.' The Latin breviary was always dear to Butler, corresponding to that little book of psalms and prayers that King Alfred had always with him. Dr. Pusey and his supporters considered that the Sarum Breviary as printed in 1531 represented the true English tradition and therefore had translations made for the use of their newly constituted communities. The Sarum use was specially suitable for Wantage, as the prebendal church had been included in the diocese of Salisbury in the days of the Benedictine Priory, and the monks would have followed the Rouen use, compiled from ancient Gallican and Latin sources, which was brought to England by St. Osmund, kinsman to William the Conqueror. The history of the Hours of Devotion, like that of the whole life of dedication, is an interesting study in itself—interesting in its continuity even when apparently extinguished. Cosin, Bishop of Durham, was to prepare a shortened form for the ladies of Charles II's court; John Austin, a recusant of the seventeenth century, produced devotions in 'the ancient way of offices', making his own beautiful psalms and producing a book that was to appear and re-appear in many forms[1] and is still published by the Wesleyans in the edition adapted by John Wesley. The ladies Miranda and Eusebia in the *Serious Call* of William Law, the friends of Thomas Ken, Lady Falkland, Lady Margaret Maynard, Mary Astell, and many others, kept the same rule of prayer.

The Founder's diary at this time has many entries such as:

July 3rd. 1848. Prime with the Sisterhood.

July 5th.   1848. Lauds with the Sisterhood ¼ to 6.

July 22nd. 1848. Kept lauds and terce with Sisterhood and addressed them shortly on their fresh beginning—may He ever prosper their work.

From Wallingford Street the Sisters moved to Newbury Street, where they began to train teachers for work in the day schools. A young pupil teacher described the simplicity of their oratory and offices: 'The oratory was an attic with a sloping roof and roughly boarded floor, the only furniture being two long desks with sloping sides made of bare deal, at which we stood to say the offices.' There is something almost reminiscent of the first Chapel of St. Clare at San Damiano, Assisi, in this little picture of the first Sisters of the Community of St. Mary the Virgin.

The day schools were not as yet finished, so that the Sisters kept school in two cottages in Mill Street; this

[1] One of the earliest forms was that of *Hickes Devotions*, which was actually compiled by Susannah Hopton who was living 'the recluse life' at Worcester.

school, with no more than twenty-four girls attending, had been in existence for some time; on the resignation of the teacher the Sisters had taken it over.

This varied activity was meeting on all sides with unexpected success, notwithstanding a certain undercurrent of suspicion; nevertheless clouds were gathering and serious trouble began to arise. The first sign of this is referred to in the Vicar's diary for 20th September, 1848: 'A note from Miss L. gave me great sorrow.' This relates to her desire to begin what was then known as penitentiary work 'among fallen girls', a work for which Henry Manning, Archdeacon of Buckingham, had conceived a great enthusiasm. This meant even more than a change from the educational aims of the original foundation. It meant that a new influence was at work and had made itself felt in the person of the Archdeacon. The Vicar, knowing himself to be in every way the Archdeacon's junior, deferred to his wishes with a heavy heart in great humility set aside his own hope of establishing a teaching order and assented to the new development. A pleasant Queen Anne house[1] was taken opposite the cottages in Newbury Street and was opened by Miss Lockhart and one of the Sisters on the lines suggested by Manning. Perhaps it was he also who advised other changes, as the Sisters next adopted a more austere rule and Miss Lockhart herself wore a monastic habit—causing the Bishop to intervene and advise the Vicar to persuade her to change it for 'a less obtrusive dress'. Butler's diary continues: 'Dec. 4th. 1848. I spoke to the Sisterhood about silence.' 'Feb. 19, 1849. Spoke to the Sisterhood on Lent.' 'April 18, 1849. Took Mr. Keble to Prime with the Sisterhood', and then, with the hint of coming trouble, 'May 16th. 1849. Visited the Sisterhood for some time. May God bless their work and give us grace

[1] This became later the nucleus of St. Mary's School.

to retain them among us. The chief difficulty was in com-
bining the two elements which naturally don't pull
together, elderly ladies who ask for a religious retreat, and
active energetic ones, like the Rev. Mother, who seem in
some sense equal, if not called to higher work.'

Opposition from outside also threatened to intervene
and obstruct. The landlord and the neighbours in Newbury Street objected to the use being made of the house,
but the Vicar, who was himself reluctant to start 'penitentiary work', won them over by his patience and understanding: 'I freely offered', he writes, 'if they really
objected to remove it elsewhere.' The objection was with-
drawn and the landlord, with his interest and sympathy
aroused, was ready to wish the work every success.

On 2nd February, 1850, Elizabeth Lockhart was
solemnly installed as Superior, but at this ceremony she
referred to the Archdeacon as 'the Father Director',
leaving the Vicar to take a secondary place. He acquiesced
humbly enough, blessing the house for the care of the
fallen instead of for the education of children, the cause
upon which he had set his heart. In the June of that year,
however, the blow fell, described in the following extract
from the Vicar's Diary.

'*June 12th, 1850.* Archdeacon Manning came. I heard
this day that Miss L. had decided on leaving the Church
of England. This is a heavy blow, but not unexpected.
Of course there was the strong influence of a mother and
brother gone,[1] and the weak support of her spiritual
adviser was little able to withstand their weight. So she
yielded. She has been a great help to us in every way,
setting before the people the sight of one seeking to fulfil
our Lord's Counsels of Perfection, and in every way being
well calculated to touch the hearts of rough thoughtless
people like ours. May He who sends this grief give us

[1] Miss Lockhart's brother was the well-known Fr. Lockhart, S.J.

strength to bear it, and save our parish from injury. It seems right to endeavour to carry on the work at any risk. The Penitents have made decided progress and it would not be right to cast them again on the world. There is every disposition on the part of Miss L. and the Archdeacon to help us in this; and I have placed all arrangements in the Bishop's hands.

'*June 16th, 1850*. Vincent went to London to see the Bishop. He returned on Saturday and with much encouragement. Barker, to whom I mentioned our position, volunteered his professional services gratis if we could continue the work. This is our first ray of light in this troubled sky.

'*June 19th, 1850*. Spent some time at St. Mary's Home, to try to arrange matters. All is unsatisfactory. The two Sisters are, to say the least, shaken, and frightened. I have mentioned this trouble to the Trinders and Pumphreys. They took it very well, sympathised much, were not turned away, as I fear some will be.

'*June 21st, 1850*. This day Miss Lockhart left us, alas, for Rome. In the afternoon the Houblons brought the Bishop of Brechin (Forbes) who gave a very deplorable account of the state of feeling in London. Men are giving up without striking a blow and lapsing into a sullen infidelity, especially in the Belgrave Square and aristocratic neighbourhoods where High Church principles have been widely sown and greedily caught. Now they say, 'we have nothing to believe.'[1] He speaks uncomfortably of the laity in Scotland as indifferent and irreligious, those belonging to the Church. May He who dwelleth on high in His Mercy hush these winds and lull these waves which rage horribly against His Church.

[1] This reaction is illuminating and is typical of English thought. Those who had welcomed revival were now led to think they had been fooled for lack of wise and informed authority.

'*February 1st, 1851.* This is the day of the week on which at this time last year the Home was opened. It returns our thoughts to the whole course of this sorrowful year, the Gorham decision, the doubts of so many, their falling from us, our own difficulties, the suspicions in which those principles are held which alone we believe to be in accordance with the Revealed Will of God. Then it is sad enough to think of the bright hopefulness with which we received Miss L. among us, the prospect of a long and useful course of work from her, our many conversations and our deep sympathies, now, alas, shivered to pieces. Still the Home has flourished with God's blessing and Vincent's constant work. And our Institutions, Schools, Services, etc. would, I am convinced, flourish also unless for our own slackness and want of energy of work and prayer. O Lord, of Thy Mercy strengthen our feeble knees and sinking hands. Let not our sinfulness mar that work which Thou hast begun among us. Make us able to cast all things else aside save the desire to serve Thee. Enable us to bear hardship as good soldiers of Christ, for His sake who died and was buried and rose again for us. I preached this evening at the Home.'

Those who followed Manning to Rome were sent by him in 1858 into the Third Order Regular of St. Francis that he had established for Mission Work in Greenwich, so that Elizabeth Lockhart never realised the enclosed vocation to which she had aspired when first shaken as to her position. The Vicar, left to face these troubles and anxieties, was still steadfast in his determination to restore the Religious Life within the English Church, but he was now subjected to the constant cry of 'No popery', accentuated by a further desertion to Rome in 1856. Placards pasted up on walls in the little tower were stealthily removed after dark by the two remaining Sisters, and it must have seemed that their whole enter-

MOTHER HARRIET

prise was doomed. Butler, on the contrary, felt himself free at last to realise his first objective of a teaching community, even if he could depend only on the two Sisters who had remained faithful through the critical disturbances; a splendid witness to his indomitable courage and faith. The two women had none of the brilliant gifts of Elizabeth Lockhart; Harriet Day was a farmer's daughter and Charlotte Gilbert was a labourer's daughter; Harriet was diffident by nature and was much afraid of the Vicar, even to disappearing when he visited the house, but she was quickly won by his patience and careful teaching. Instruction took place every day in his study; he was determined that whatever structure might eventually rise, the foundations must be sound, deep and laid with the utmost care.

The little household set itself to pray for a Superior with great simplicity of heart, little thinking that Harriet was the one chosen by God to mother the growing family for thirty-four years. She was installed on 21st February, 1854, under a form adapted from the Latin *Benedictio Abbatissale*. Though Butler was clear that nothing should now interfere with his educational plans, he had no intention of dropping the 'penitentiary work' having once set his hand to the plough. He did not of course live to see the new call to service that lay before the community —in recent years the Sisters have had the pride and inspiration of working with and for the State under the Home Office in their moral welfare work.

Eight years after the days of trial the Founder could remind his growing community of all the difficulties that had been surmounted by the grace of God. 'Certain it is, that there has been no great, good and abiding work that did not seem at one time in risk and peril, whose progress was not slow and gradual. You will find the same story of small beginnings with slight indications of support and yet sufficient for the faithful heart to feel that 'the still, small voice' was in those small indications, guiding him, cherishing and upholding him for greater things and for more complete success . . . In His good time, perfecting, stablishing, strengthening, sealing you, He shall give you the consolation of a manifold blessing. "Yea, the Lord shall increase you more and more, you and your children." ' Butler's own birthday fell on St. Scholastica's day, 10th February, and he wrote about this time to his sister drawing her attention to his Benedictine patroness, adding: 'The name seems well adapted to my line of work;' but the rule that he chose for the community was not that of St. Benedict.

In 1860 he was given permission by the Canons Regular of Tepl near Marienbad to transcribe the Latin Rule of St. Augustine, a work he accomplished by sitting up all night in their library. This was translated and adapted later by Canon Liddon and others, and from that and other sources, notably the writings of St. François de Sales, who had brought the Visitation under the same rule, the present rule of the community was compiled, pointing the way along which the Sisters were to travel. The rule of St. Augustine as contained in his letters to the Abbess Felicitas is one of principles rather than injunctions, simple and elastic, available for the contemplative, active or mixed life.

In the great revival of the religious congregations in France during the seventeenth and eighteenth centuries especial emphasis was given to the contrasted work of Martha and Mary, at the moment when the call had come for nuns to undertake active work, re-entering the world in a return to the function of leaven, a vocation that is so constantly needed when faith is shaken. This awakening influenced contemporary English thought to an amazing extent—libraries like those of Ken and Law contain the works of St. François de Sales, early studies were made of St. Vincent de Paul, of Nicholas Pavillon of Alet and the Spanish mystics. This study was continued by the Tractarians and the first dress of our early religious communities resembles those of the *Regents* of Alet or *Les Filles d'Instruction* rather than those of German deaconesses. Yet unwilling as Butler was to dictate to his small Community, he held himself 'willing, should it be the Divine Providence, that the contemplative life should have freedom of development'. The Rule of St. Augustine and the French ideal of the twofold life of Martha and Mary opened the way for them to wait upon the guidance of the Holy Spirit as well as to experiment in an active life. Therefore, we find in Butler's definition of the aim set before his community that in addition to the primary work of rescue and education, 'the Community shall be free according to the words of the Blessed Virgin Mary: "Whatsoever He saith unto you, do it", to undertake any service of prayer or active work to which it may be led.' In addressing the little society in 1849 he had said: 'To serve in Martha's special work, to contemplate in Mary's —Martha provides that Mary may have leisure to gaze. Mary could not contemplate did not Martha serve. Mary's eye must be for internal things if Martha cares most for external. Martha purchases, arranges, helps; for she serves, works, buys, holds, dispenses for the love of Christ. Hence she will serve from morning till evening that others may enjoy His Beloved Presence. The two characters form a perfect whole—each may, neither need, fail.'

In this 'mixed life' that Butler had visualised for his Sisters, he loved as usual to give full scope to character and individuality. To him, by a seeming paradox, obedience and free personality were one; self-emptying in his mind was one with self-fulfilment, 'obedience', he declared, 'was freedom.' There must be scope for Martha's active brain and she must be free to spend housekeeping money as she judged best, as well as to be spent herself in service. And to Mary's self-emptying in recollection, he would add beauty in worship, for grace must bring grace or it denies itself. Where everything was kept in deliberate and almost Cistercian simplicity he gave every encouragement to music, making it part of the Sisters' life of worship. Butler had a great understanding and love of plain chant and all other church music, saying that, 'Catholic music like Catholic words must affect Catholic hearts. Indeed it is a true and component part of Catholic teaching.' This led him to a search for good instructors, but 'Mr. Helmore tells me there is no mission spirit among the younger men'. Failing other leaders, however, Butler managed to inculcate such a love for plain chant in the hearts of the community that it has been allowed to become a centre of production consulted by many, printing all the music in use and counting it as a chief part of its work of worship and offering to God. In all this it was guided by the careful researches of Dr. George Palmer among museum manuscripts and all ancient sources.

In 1856, with a real sense of stability and assurance, the Sisters, now increasing in numbers, moved into their first Convent set on the Limburh of King Alfred's day.[1] Consciously or unconsciously their founder had also linked the community with the Saxon Chapel of St. Mary in the churchyard, by placing them under the protection of St. Mary the Virgin and bidding them hold her five festivals in special veneration, the five festivals for which

[1] A Captain Symonds who visited Wantage in 1644 wrote, 'upon ye North West Side of ye towne on a rising hill, is ye olde seate of the family of Fitz Warin, who lived there and had been the habitation of King Alfred. But was no mention of any ruines.'

indulgences had been granted in the old Saxon Church. This link was not only a religious one, for the Chapel, having later become the home of the early Latin School, also sealed their vocation as teachers.

The new Convent must have appeared a veritable paradise to the small company; it was beautifully situated, convenient according to the standards of the day, and not unlike an old manor house in its design; in any case it gave them their hearts' desire. Their spiritual life centred round a tiny temporary chapel of period Gothic, now used as a room named Help. Speaking to them there, the Founder told his humble daughters: 'Very wholesome it is for us in our simple unadorned and formless household to give thanks to God that we see not yet our reward. It must be good for us, it is like our Lord Himself and, believe me, we need not fear. Fear not little flock, it is His own gracious word. The little one in God's good time shall become a thousand.'[1]

Again speaking to the Sisters in 1873 he reminds them of the mark of their Community much in the manner of St. François de Sales in his addresses to the Sisters of the Visitation.

'The distinguishing characteristic of this Society has, from the first, been simplicity. Our object at the beginning was to gather together those who would be content with a frugal life, patient toil, quiet appearance, content with yielding themselves in simple-hearted devotion to spend and be spent for their Master and their Lord. I repeat, great simplicity in dress and, if I may use the word, in ritual. Hard work and little show has ever been the mark of this Community. Does this seem an unsatisfactory aim?

[1] The rapid growth of the Community did not take place until after the Founder's death. It was as if his strong will had to be held on a firm rein, but that his prayer, released in death, was acceptable in the sight of God.

Surely not! If we consider Him who was "the lowly" as well as "the undefiled one". Is not this hidden life the ideal of the true Sister? And where can she find it sooner than in extreme simplicity, a quiet exterior and in deep humility?' At the time he was speaking the Community was beginning to develop the more ordered life of the old Priory, while retaining the simplicity of the yet older Domrahamme. Firm in the English tradition, they were to draw many to their family and household, gradually gaining the confidence of Church and people and thus proving themselves to be loyal to their spiritual and national inheritance and not an alien foundation that gave its allegiance elsewhere.

Writing to the Associates of the Community in 1878 Mother Harriet said: 'The principle of English Sisterhoods is on its trial, and we feel keenly how greatly by one error or false step we might injure that for which we have given our lives.'

Chapter Three

THE STREAM OF ENGLISH TRADITION

The English tradition whether in Church, national life, or individual character, has always been marked by action, under-statement and reserve. Although self-depreciatory and usually inarticulate, the ordinary Englishman is ready for self-sacrifice and even martyrdom without any apparent realisation that anything out of the ordinary has been demanded of him. 'My opportunity come along and I took it and if it come along again I hope to take it again', was the shy explanation of the East-ender V.C. in the 1914 war. In every department of English life it is the active and practical that has predominated; even the English Mystics are noted for their simplicity and direct reality.

This 'happy breed of men' persists down the centuries, bringing with it the same characteristic, constructive, patient outlook, the same desire to keep a balance, the same silence, foresight and discrimination. Wantage in the seventeenth century gave birth to just such an Englishman, a man of conscience, judgment and devotion. Joseph Butler, subsequently Bishop of Durham, was born in the Priory Cottage within Priors Hold in 1692. He is in the Alfredian succession because he was so English, so gravely devoted to God, so concentrated on education and social work. As a boy he attended the small Latin School in the Churchyard, once the ancient Church of St. Mary, and eventually as Dean of St. Paul's appointed his old schoolmaster to the first living in his gift as a mark of gratitude. Born of Presbyterian parents who attended the Baptist Chapel in Wantage, he deliberately chose as a boy to attend the Church services and though later educated at a Nonconformist school for their ministry, he was firm in his decision for ordination in the Church, having been influenced by his friend Edward Talbot, Vicar of East Hendred near Wantage, the son of the Bishop of Salisbury. He was ordained by the Bishop, Wantage being then in the diocese of Salisbury, and lived to become in due course Dean of St. Paul's, Bishop of Bristol and Bishop of Durham; but was yet more renowned as the author of 'the Analogy', a reasoned argument for faith in a period of darkness and widespread unbelief.

By speech, writing and sermon Joseph Butler forced men to realise their need of faith, churchmanship, evangelisation and education. His defence of medical benefits for the poor and widespread educational opportunity might meet even modern criticisms of social advance; he pressed home the duties and obligations of Christians that must extend beyond their own nation to those employed in foreign countries, colonies and to native populations. He even made an appeal, as Bishop of Bristol, to Dissenters to join in such a work and ought to have met with a better response from Wesley or Whitfield, to whom he had showed consideration.[1] Bishop Butler was as careful of money as his great Wantage predecessor, spending as dutifully on house property and position as Alfred spent on his Court, yet, with Alfred, setting aside very large sums for spiritual and educational work. It is characteristic that in his portrait as Bishop of Durham he holds the plan of the Newcastle Infirmary to which he gave £400 a year. In one of his sermons preached in 1747 after the rising in '45, Butler, himself a strong

[1] It is strange that Wesley held himself aloof from Butler's overtures; collaboration might at this point have saved a cleavage in the Church; it certainly helps to absolve the Church from the charge of total neglect of those overseas.

Hanoverian, speaks boldly on the necessity of Constitutional Government as the safeguard of freedom and security so that men may 'realise the reasonable aim of their life on earth'. It is an approach to the conception of a democracy, even if his times were not as yet wholly ripe for this.

His great charge to the Durham clergy in 1751 lays down the principles of the English tradition in parochial life, a pastoral ideal governed by careful reverence and catholic usage in all things appertaining to worship; but he was none the less bold to point out that 'in Roman Catholic countries people cannot pass a day without having religion recalled to their thought by some or other memorial of it, by some ceremony or public religious form occurring in their way, beside the very frequent Holy days, the short prayers they are called on to say and the occasional devotions enjoined by confessors'. This and the fact that he had placed a white marble cross on a black marble ground behind the altar in his Chapel at Bristol brought upon him the usual accusations of popery, one writer saying that 'he has squinted very much towards that superstition'. The Bishop remained unperturbed by such attacks, keeping himself somewhat aloof from the strife of tongues and still encouraging his clergy to follow a methodical ministry of souls and 'the keeping up of the form and face of religion with decency and reverence'. Once again and from Wantage we find a man, as a pitcher, carrying the waters of spiritual life, sound education and an English tradition to refresh the troubled spirit of his generation. Bishop Butler was a true precursor of Newman and Keble, who expressed their obligation to him and acknowledged that their 'whole cast of thought and method' was determined by his writings.

Writing from Hursley in 1846, Mr. Keble pointed out to William John Butler 'the good omen' of his appointment to the living where he might become 'a second Butler of Wantage'. To this William John answered 'I am not quite sure whether "Butler of Wantage" is not a calculation of chances against me—one would suppose that it would exhaust the powers of Wantage to produce Butlers and that future Butlers would be the poorest of their species'.

In handling the difficult parish committed to him Butler the Second was clear as to the English pastoral ideal. He insisted on the parochial visiting of the clergy, and he had usually a staff of five curates, quoting the old saying that the house-going parson makes a church-going people. 'Nothing at all', he added, 'no fine preaching, nor overflowing soup kitchen, nor system of assiduous "district visitors" brings the people to church like the regular, loving visit of the parson.' This was 'to gain a real knowledge of the people's minds and natures, their weaknesses and strong points, their needs of body and soul . . . not the least even their language, varying as it does in many parts of England and, as all know, so closely interwoven with their mode of thought'. As he wrote, taught and practised this, he must have become well acquainted with the Durham Charge, for he is apt to quote Butler the First and not only Butler but Langton, Grossetête, Parker, Laud, More, Strafford, Falkland and Evelyn as well as his contemporaries Pusey, Keble, Selwyn, Harrington and Gray. While keeping the junior clergy close to the 'grind' of his aphorism, he well knew that faith and prayer were the actual essentials and that the end in view must always be 'the winning of souls to Christ and the maintaining them in the right course'. 'The winning of souls must resemble the taking of a city. Trenches must be laid down, often far from the walls, gradually to approach nearer and nearer until the opportunity is found of entering.' With this outlook he had little use for short cuts or dogmatic assertions or any arbitrary interpretation of sacerdotalism. He knew his nation too well, he cared for God's honour too much. Father Noel of St. Barnabas, Oxford, who had served under him as curate, was advised to avoid 'all things irritating', as the battle was too serious, too vital. They were 'out to deprotestantise a nation' as Butler described it, not because he had any quarrel with the evangelical view of life, but because in indifferent, unbelieving days the word 'protestantism' had become a cover to avoid effort and to block progress. The 'No popery' cry was actually an escape from self-knowledge, responsibility and reform. Many of his curates attained to eminence—Dr. Liddon, Father Maconochie, Father Noel, Canon Newbolt, Canon Stuckey Coles, Father Longridge, C.R., and Father Maxwell, Superior General of the Society of St. John the Evangelist. The curates lived together in the Priory, there linked with the Benedictines and with Joseph Butler, and he made each of them responsible for a definite district or one of the adjacent villages. They met daily at the Vicarage at 1.15, first in the oratory or prayer room for Sext and None, afterwards dining with the family, followed by conference in the study. Their mornings had to be given to prayer and meditation, the afternoons were devoted to visiting. 'The curates' are remembered as wearing 'cassocks and tall hats in the morning and tail coats in the afternoon. When asked by one if they must always wear top hats the Vicar replied laughing "My dear fellow, if the clergy were to alter their hats the Church tower would fall down." ' Years after, his successor was to give the clergy leave to wear soft 'shovel' hats, but on the first day that this reckless revolution had taken place the Verger had to report to the Vicar that a crack had appeared in the Church tower.

Though Butler's demands were exacting he is described

by all who really knew him as 'always ready to wait'. His curates witnessed to this: they were more impressed by 'the patience with which the Vicar waited' than by anything else, a patience that extended to individual souls and very markedly to his opponents. Indeed those who worked most closely with him recognised 'his deep undemonstrative love, bent upon the single-hearted service of God', and 'his joyous nature, the ceaseless activity of his life, his tender compassionate sympathy, his strong will subdued to God'. Father Pollock of St. Albans wrote, 'I never met one in a position with whom one was so absolutely at one's ease, sure of his warm kindness of heart. He never "pawed" people either with words or hands; he had stronger and more manly ways of showing affection.' Many learned from him 'that the word comfort means strength and think of him as, above all, a very Barnabas of consolation'. He was forebearing in his consideration for the feelings and prejudices of the people and was gentle in word and deed, even if he were 'very plain spoken and somewhat stern when things were done which ought not to have been done, and still more when things were omitted that ought to have been done'. One opponent said bluntly, 'I do not know whether you are most knave or fool.' 'Time will show', answered the Vicar tolerantly, 'time will show.'

The constant going forth into the parish to establish contact, friendship and guidance was to find its counterpart in as constant a drawing into the centre in warmhearted hospitality and for the purpose of instruction and building up the good work begun outside. The Vicar's classes were numberless; it is difficult to understand how an over-worked man could gather together concentration and welcome, to say nothing of wits, as group succeeded group in his study. 'During the week preceding a general Communion, he gave eleven or twelve classes to the

Communicants at hours which were convenient to each group and in order that no maid-servant should miss the chance of attending he arranged for two classes at different times for those in domestic service. There was a class for bellringers, for the farmers, for the women of the almshouses, for the Grammar schoolboys, in fact for everyone. His study was tightly packed with chairs and those who had no chair sat on the floor. He delighted in these classes, calling them "the very life blood of the parish." '

This high standard of pastoral work led Butler to the conviction that there was both need and opening for Community houses for secular priests, living, as at Hippo, the celibate life, in strict obedience to the Prayer Book with its daily worship, frequent Communion and round of fasts and festivals. Such houses he would place under direct episcopal supervision and 'the dress of the members should not be peculiar or demonstrative and the diet plain but sufficient': dispensable vows of poverty, chastity and obedience should be taken, but he did not intend that his plan should necessarily cover life vocations. This recurrent need in the English Church was early foreseen by him, but he had neither time nor money to carry his scheme into execution; his energy was absorbed elsewhere.

His patience must have been sorely tried while awaiting a moment for the restoration of the Parish Church. Schools and ground work had to take precedence, but Butler's whole outlook and temperament must have longed to put the Church first. The fabric had been badly neglected and obtrusive galleries in which none of the appointments were worthy or beautiful had been thrust into the building. He was from the outset careful that nothing cheap or meretricious should be allowed entrance and his work, in an age of rash renovation, may be counted as cultured and conservative; that there was some loss was almost inevitable, for we have to remember

that it was the era of the Great Exhibition, of ingenuous
Gothic and unnecessary ornament.[1] Butler was saved by
his own innate taste and by his concentration on worship
as the ultimate end of restoration. All his arrangements
'bore a striking witness to the Real Presence'. He did not
hesitate to regret the ruling of the English Church that,
at that time, made reservation impossible, 'but he taught
his Sisters to practise adoration for some moments before
Communion and added a daily memorial of Corpus
Christi to their ferial vespers'. The daily offices of Matins
and Evensong were sung with severe adherence to plain
chant, not only for the psalms, but, on weekdays, for the
hymns also, which were those translated from the Latin
by Dr. Neale. The parochial Eucharist on Sunday was
always sung at such an hour that would not preclude
Communion. In regard to this Butler had been greatly
interested to find that the tradition among the simpler
country folk was to receive their Communion 'leer'—
fasting; other traditional observances he notes in his diary
among the inhabitants of Charlton, an outlying hamlet—
that 'the poor are rough and low in their ways but simple-
hearted. . . . They have but a formular notion of religion
yet sometimes this formula helps one on to Catholic
observance. . . . It is remarkable that while the more
respectable inhabitants of Wantage seem to care little for
a clergyman's administrations in time of sickness, these
Charlton people hold a traditionary regard for such'.

It is surprising to learn that the Vicar approved of
Communion on Good Friday, saying that it was not
possible for most people to bear the burden of long

---

[1] It was not until Butler was appointed Dean of Lincoln that he
was able to give full rein to his love for beauty and order; there he
restored the neglected retro-choir of the Cathedral to its ancient
beauty. He assigned every Chapel to a special use to be fully realised
at the present time.

watches and fasts without Communion. In this he proved himself curiously in line with the earliest form of the Mass of the Pre-sanctified, which had included the Communion of the faithful. But even without knowledge of this historic fact, Butler was so acutely aware of the pressure of evil and the powers arrayed against religion that he was loth indeed to weaken any simple approach to God. It was characteristic of his own reverent approach that he re-instated the houseling cloth at all large Communions.

One of the earliest scholars of St. Mary's School looks back across more than seventy years to describe the Church services. 'Matins was beautifully sung early every morning and Evensong every evening at 7 p.m., at which the St. Mary's School Girls used to be present together with the teachers, girls and mistresses of St. Michael's. Among the parishioners "blind Sally", an old woman who had been taught the whole Psalter by one of the clergy, and all the office hymns used during the course of the year. She used to sing everything in an old quavering voice but quite correctly. Two old men used also to come to Evensong; they wore linen smocks.'

The rigour of the Prayer Book was seldom relaxed, even when the Prince and Princess of Wales (King Edward VII and Queen Alexandra) came to Wantage in 1877 for the unveiling of the statue of King Alfred in the Market Square; they were not exempted from full choral Matins. It is true that they were allowed to choose the hour and they named 12 noon. The Church was decked for festival, and the Vicar preached an eloquent sermon on King Alfred—at the end of which, it is remembered, he paused and, looking directly at the Prince, said distinctly: 'Go and do *thou* likewise.'

Standing as an English Churchman amongst Englishmen and ever faithful to the English tradition, Butler was never insular or narrow but staunchly Catholic, and he had a special admiration for the religious revival after the wave of atheism and deism on the continent. He spoke French and German fluently, so that his many journeys abroad were made easy, and he could enter at once into understanding and friendship with the people. This colloquial at-homeness brought him as an eager visitor, most courteously welcomed to many religious houses abroad, and he delighted to seek out ecclesiastics and monastics from whom he was ready to learn all that was possible. Arguments seldom arose on these occasions. Butler had no wish for controversy, but if need be he could stand firm, yet always with a friendly sense of humour. 'Soyez conséquent, monsieur,' said his monastic host to him one day, 'soyez conséquent,' to which he replied, 'Les Anglais sont toujours inconséquents.'

It was his joy and privilege to spend hours within the convents and monasteries of active religious, studying their buildings, their rule of life, their work and worship. Writing of *les petites Sœurs des pauvres* to his wife he says, 'If I were converted it would be by such sights as that, not by the good Father's arguments and eloquence;' and again, 'I could have cried with delight at what I saw and heard.' This experience of friendly interchange without change on either side was accentuated and deepened when Butler volunteered for Red Cross service in the Franco-Prussian War in 1870, and went forth under the most sordid conditions to minister to both French and German wounded at Saarbrücken, Sedan and elsewhere. He met and cheered Charles Wood, afterwards Lord Halifax, in the Red Cross at Sedan. In this adventure, one much after his heart, he was thrown together with many French nuns, as also with the Mother and Sisters of the English Community of All Saints, so that he was able to write of his work, 'It really seems to lift one above the earth,' and again, 'I cannot help smiling some-

ABOUT 1880

times at myself and my work, yet really I think that there is some satisfaction in finding that I can do what I am told to do. Sometimes I have feared that my masterful nature had no humility in it, but I am nearly sure that want of humility is not my special fault.'

The days of social service had barely dawned and Butler was before his time when he volunteered for war work, but his social energies did not end there. Colonel Lord Wantage, V.C., his friend and neighbour, spoke of the patriotism 'that was a marked feature of his singularly manly character. He was an Englishman and a patriot to his heart's core', and he continued by describing Butler, as Regimental Chaplain to the Berkshire Volunteers, celebrating for them in a tent set on the downs, or preaching stirring sermons on *Scutchmanob*[1] with its ancient Saxon tumulus. The Vicar wrestled with outbreaks of typhoid, had insanitary property cleared, was foremost in the introduction of a tram service to the station, the work of macadamising the roads, the installation of gas and the organisation of the local trade; while, like his great namesake Butler the first, he inaugurated the scheme for a local hospital. Even when it was impossible to work these diverse and multitudinous plans out himself in detail, his neighbours recognised that it was the Vicar's eager incentive that had dispersed their lethargy and had roused them to reform. He saw life as a whole, he held his office as a trust from God for the people, his house was open house, and he moved amongst his parishioners as a friend; secular and sacred were indivisible to him to whom all was sacred. In a word he was the Parson as well as the priest, the willing person of the parish. We do not need to press the point that he was a worthy heir to the great men before him; he was in a succession that engendered success.

[1] The local rendering of "Cwichelmslaw."

Chapter Four

'BLOSSOM GATHERINGS'

Alfred in the ninth century made selections from the Soliloquies of St. Augustine for the devout persons of that age, collecting them together under the charming title of *Blossom Gatherings*. William John Butler also gathered blossoms from the same garden when he gave his community St. Augustine's rule of life. Now in these latter times we fill our smaller jar with petals and flowers that are garnered from the first beginnings of the Founder's work, in order that some of the fragrance may be wafted to us from those early days. A character is as often revealed by chance sayings and passing acts as by more important pronouncements and works; we are more closely drawn to a man by his daily life than by outstanding episodes. So the Sisters and young teachers trained by Butler have treasured trivial memories revealing the man: these make him live again for later generations and come down to us in all their original freshness and wit, that may well go deeper than graver words. Many, now well over seventy, recall reminiscences of the nursery garden plot at St. Michael's of which they speak with happy gratitude, and they bring simple little bouquets which are none the less sweet. One has an amusing memory of the Vicar's love for plain, honest speech. He had had an accident to his leg and a young teacher who was to drive with him to the station was reminded by the Sister Superior 'to mind and ask after his leg'. But this was beyond the courage and convention of the refined young lady in those days of early Victorian bashfulness and she therefore gave the message that 'Sister Bessie wants to know how your foot is'; on which the Vicar with quick retort, exclaimed, 'You know she said nothing of the sort, tell me what she did say,' following it up with a witty little reprimand on false modesty. He was most particular as to speech and behaviour during the repetition of the Catechism, so, to a boy who lolled carelessly when repeating his answer, the Vicar said sharply: 'Stand up properly on your own hind legs. God has given you a good pair of legs and you should stand on them.' He expected the girls of St. Mary's School to keep their eyes on him when giving a lesson and to remain attentive no matter what happened. 'I don't want to speak to the tops of pates', he said, and, 'If I bring an elephant and march it up and down, the children ought not to take their eyes off their work.' But he made the one exception of a Bishop's visit. 'You may look up and pay attention if there are gaiters.' When a child in the Sunday School repeated 'my dooty towards God' with a strong Berkshire accent, the Vicar was delighted. 'That's it,' he exclaimed, 'I like to hear you say that good old word "Dooty", for dooty is what we have to do.'

Hardly a detail escaped a very quick observant eye; once when starting for one of their long walks it is remembered that the Vicar discovered that there were buttons off a girl's boot. He promptly sent the owner back to her room again to sew on the buttons, but did not fail to tell her of a short cut by which to catch up the party. There was usually a kindly postscript to a reprimand and Butler could not bear to leave an impression of fear.

He was careful of manners, telling the girls to take pains to find the right initials when writing to a clergyman. 'You must never put "the reverend ——". Dash is a dog's name.' Once he rebuked a novice saying, 'I heard you say something last night that I beg you will never say again; you were warning the girls with "Now, what would the Vicar say?'' Never hold me up as a terror before them, love is better than fear.' He did not wait to hear the trembling explanation that her question was actually on a point of doctrine. No one could doubt, however, that he was in authority and exercised it to the full. For instance, another young novice who was then teaching in the school had often been late for tea after being detained by the Vicar. The Novice Mistress therefore intervened, putting her under obedience to be punctual. In consequence of this she hurried away from school and ignored a call from the Vicar to stop, but when he continued she had to explain that she was under orders to be punctual. This was quickly swept aside with the words, 'I am above Sister Mary',—and that was that, as a later generation would say. On the other hand, a novice emerging from the cellar stairs with both hands laden met, with some confusion, a courteous, tall gentleman who made her a reverent bow of deep respect, conveying to her mind, at once, a sense of the honour she possessed as a handmaid of the Lord.

We are told that when the Founder opened the door of the Embroidery Room he always said 'The Lord be with you', and those present would answer 'And with thy spirit'. The Embroidery Room played an important part in the revival of worship. The altar frontals of those early years are still in use in the parish church and elsewhere; they follow strict tradition, but are bold in design and colour and are quite uninfluenced by the contemporary love of passion flowers and tendrils. The more delicate revival of medieval art came later, with accurate historic detail, skilful figure design and varied stitchery. Canon Law had provided that the Altar should be always covered by 'a decent carpet', and the neglect of this had contributed to a 'careless indifference as to the form and face of religion', to quote Bishop Butler, which assisted the decay of religion itself. An old Sister, one of the more famous among the embroideresses, used to claim that she had found her vocation through a visit paid in her youth to a West Norfolk church. Finding no altar at all in the church, she asked the reason for its absence and was told that there was a cricket match on and it had been taken out for use as a scoring table. Agnes Blencoe exclaimed in horror that if that altar had had its 'decent carpet' no one would have dared to use it for such a purpose, and from that moment she offered her life in reparation.

One of the first of the St. Mary's School girls recollects, in her old age, that the Vicar was as firm and original in his artistic convictions as in most things. His taste certainly inclined to the primitive and medieval, for she remembers him stamping his foot to add emphasis to a 'Perish Michael Angelo and perish Raphael' declaimed for the benefit of the girls. But that too was both honest and bold, as well as original, in the early days of Queen Victoria.

His daughter pictures his hurried meals, almost invariably accompanied by an interview or an obligato of arrangements and orders. 'I never remember him having any exceptional food, but I do remember his hatred of melted butter and of his saying once of a friend that he never ate an egg unless he knew the hen.' That morning his egg had made itself known without introduction. Yet whatever happened he had always time, time for reading the French exercises of a girl he was trying to encourage, time for visiting, time for entering into the joys and sorrows of others, time to observe and time to help. To the Sisters who were in charge of children he impressed the need of plenty of tubbing, plenty of games, plenty of fun and brightness and plenty of jam. If the sacristan had a cold he gave her lozenges; to a girl who was burdened by having the sole charge of her father's house he gave money 'to buy a blue ribbon', while commending her devotion to her home and family; whenever special events occurred in his schools the children had to take the news straight to the Vicarage and 'great was his delight if any one had a distinction, especially if it happened to be in Divinity'. Once a girl named Agnes came to consult him about entering the religious life. He said, 'How old are you?' and when she answered 'Seventeen' he replied, 'Go home and play with the lambs in the fields for another two years and then, perhaps, come and see me again.'

He never lacked courage and, commenting on the anger of a man whom he had reproved for sin, he wrote: 'He is very angry with me. People of that kind have been so little found fault with for doing wrong by a minister that it seems presumptouous to them when one does one's duty.' He even reproved women for unsuitability of dress—an interesting problem for discussion in these present times and one that requires careful and unprejudiced thought. He urged one woman to 'great simplicity of manner and dress as the best mode of influencing those with whom she has to deal, whose frivolity and smallness of aim she herself can see and deplore'. He spoke to a newly confirmed girl who was showing 'inordinate vanity and love of dress'. She owned, 'I got no good from Confirmation because I went there with a half heart. I was thinking all the time about the crêpe dress.' 'Poor child', he added, 'may God open her eyes.' Of another he wrote 'I'm afraid she talks too much to be real'.

A hawker came to him asking for Baptism and the diary tells us, 'I fear he has very little idea what he seeks, he is a rough ignorant man. But what can be expected after a life of hawking, spent in low fairs and the like?

If he be baptised, which God grant, he must be carefully prepared.' Another hawker was willing to be prepared for Communion; the difficulty in his case was 'the chaffering and dealing which, as he says, involves much lying'.

The Vicar was very particular as to the reverent administration of Holy Baptism, and spoke seriously to sponsors, teaching them beforehand every word of their part in the service. Baptising 'a tramper's child' in 1850, he writes: 'the parents alone being sponsors. This was, of course, extra rubrical, but we had no resource except to send the child away unbaptised or to baptise it privately which would have been equally a breach of discipline. Of course it would be better if we could gather together a few to take the part of sponsors when either none can be obtained or unfit only.' He is pleased to record that after careful instruction 'Mrs. B's little girl baptised by her parents wish, the second Sunday after birth. This was very satisfactory'.

Never once did he relax watchfulness; before he had been in Wantage a year he noticed: 'I fear me that an idle spirit is *returning* on this Parish. Gossip is a point to be worked at.' His class of big lads had been also getting slack. 'These big lads', he writes, 'are the most difficult portion of the Parish to keep in good ways. Their bodies and passions are strong and they are not calculating enough to feel the restraint of society and interest which keep others within bounds. They live without respect for God or man. They cannot feel Church or prayers or understand arguments. They can be led neither by fear or love. It is quite clear that something can or ought to be done. Teach us what things we ought to do in this case, O Lord!' Instead of warnings or inhibitions: 'I must try to lay before them the blessedness of an holy life in the hope that under God's blessing this may kindle or call into action that spark of Baptismal life which we may hope is not yet extinguished in creatures so young.' A novice recollects that one day, when walking with the Vicar, they watched some boys playing leapfrog. One small boy shirked his leap, so Butler went back and made him try again with good success. On rejoining his companion he said, 'There, that will do him good for the rest of his life, when shirking would have done him harm.' Sports, games, walks, van outings to interesting places, all helped to lighten the tillage of faith, grind and prayer. 'I believe they are as likely as anything', the diary tells us, 'to raise a good spirit in the minds of young people.'

Some of the farmers who had attended one of Butler's celebrated classes came to him to ask for Confirmation. In recording this he writes on 6th February, 1850. 'Dined with the farmers, the anniversary of their markets. They sent to ask me and, in proposing the health of P and myself, spoke most heartily of their affection for the Church. I believe that all or almost all our middle class strength is among these men, and that if we could only add intelligence to their inborn feeling for the institutions of the land, they would form an important barrier to the latitudinarianism of the manufacturing and mechanical classes. I spoke to them on the need of "manuring their minds".' On the other hand he complains constantly of the lack of church attendance among tradesmen and their wives, 'wandering about in morning service,' and of how little impression he has been able to make upon them. Later he records with pleasure the presence of 'respectables' at an evening service on Midsummer Day (St. John the Baptist) and writes 'I am scheming to have my classes higher up in society'. He was to be greatly rewarded by the loyalty of such people as his ministry developed, and by the leading part they were to play in the life of the parish.

There was, on occasion, an almost Shakespearian sense of humour in his dealing with men. One fair day he found a notorious drinker dead drunk. He took away his trousers, knowing he had only the one pair, and this caught the man's sense of humour and started a real friendship; he used to be seen afterwards, walking with the Vicar, hanging on to his arm in friendship and not because there was need of support. Charlton Feast, kept at Whitsuntide, proved a counter attraction to the Church services and a strong temptation to the people. 'The only plan is to *clinch* the communicants and gather them round to pray for the others. O Lord grant us Thy help to do Thy Will; make us prayerful, loving, earnest in season and out of season.'

Whatever happened, whatever anxieties weighed on his scrupulous mind, he loved the people and love is bound to win in the end. He rejoiced in the smocked frocks still worn, in the old men bravely wearing 'Welsh Wigs' on a Sunday because a draper in the town had lately sold off his stock cheap, those old men some of whom 'have so long attended the daily service and are now drawing on to the Blessed Sacrament to which some little time ago they expressed repugnance'. He wants to 'enclose all kinds of fishes and bring them into God's service, toning down yet without destroying the savour of their individuality'. Perhaps that is why he delighted in telling the story of the man who was once overheard in his efforts to explain a miracle to a friend: 'Well, supposin' you was to wake up at 12 o'clock in the middle of the night and see the sun shinin' into your winder what would you say then?' The other answered stolidly, 'I'd say it was the moon.' 'But', persisted his friend, 'supposin' you knew it *wasn't* the moon, what would you say then?' 'I'd say', replied Berkshire quite firmly, 'it was time to get up.' It is possible that a much loved Mother General of his Community had caught something of his own spirit when, rousing herself on her deathbed, she said 'You haven't told me who won the boat race'.

Chief among many friends was Charlotte Yonge, and Butler kept her photograph on his mantelpiece. She used to come every year on a visit to the Vicarage, and she wrote the impressions of her first visit to a friend: 'When I first knew Wantage the principal improvements were already established and nothing struck me so much as the zest, life and spirit which pervaded everything, the early Service, the merry breakfast, the schools, the Parish visiting, the mid-day dinner with the Curates, the various claims on the afternoon, the classes, the evening visits to parishioners so as to see men and boys, the Evensong with a Sermon twice a week, all concluded by a supper as lively as the former meals had been; all came in quick succession, and there was something brilliant and quaint about all . . . the Vicarage is before my mind—the mullioned windows of the dining room festooned with creepers, a shady walk leading to the churchyard bordered with limes and skirting a lawn. It was a place of general hospitality for gentle and simple, where endless deep discussions and merry jokes might go on among old and young, specially after supper when the day's work was done, and its humours could be related. Playfulness was a great element in the household and . . . Mrs. Butler's[1] strong sense of the ridiculous had been a great safeguard against eccentricities of ritual, when so much was experimental and Curates were hot-headed and theoretical. There was certainly an uncompromising contempt of

[1] Charles, Lord Halifax, in recalling the books of his childhood, writes: '*Sintram* and *Undine* by La Motte Fouqué, in the translation never since equalled, much less surpassed, of Mrs. Butler the wife of Dean Butler of Wantage and Lincoln.' Quoted on p. 29 of Lord Halifax's *Life*, pt. i.

nonsense, and therewith of unreal sentiment, and there were some who could not stand the ordeal of irony. The atmosphere was a good deal like a brisk frosty morning, excellent and enjoyable to the active and energetic, but a severe test to the weaker or to those who thought charity akin to indifference to evil. Simple folly was borne with, humbug never tolerated.'[1]

Miss Yonge also speaks of his decision that the Community should never 'beg', and adds that 'the Wantage Sisters have never done this and they have thriven'. She describes the long expeditions that the Vicar loved and in which she joined, and recalls that, when he was offered the living, Butler had said he wished that he could find a wise old curate not to work but to advise.

A 'Butler rule' that still obtains at St. Mary's School, except on very rare occasions, was that of spending Easter where Holy Week had been kept so as not to break into the sequence of the great happenings. His own plan was to return to Wantage[2] for that period, but when he became Dean of Lincoln, where the statutes of the Cathedral required him to preach on Easter Day, he was obliged to leave on Holy Saturday. On returning from Worcester or Lincoln a Sister recalls: 'people came long distances to make their Confessions and the hard pressed Dean had to meet a continual stream from early morning until 7.30 p.m. If there was a pause he would be found on his knees before his writing table trying to finish letters.[3] On one very busy day, at another time, a Sister actually

[1] *Life and Letters of Dean Butler*, Chap. IX, p. 206. Macmillan.

[2] It is interesting that when he returned his place of residence was The Mead, then in the possession of old friends, thus linking him once again with the past, the distant past—Alfred, the Domrahamme and Fitzwarin.

[3] The Founder described himself to an Associate who visited Lincoln as 'always busy but never tired'.

found him reading a story, but he held up a finger as she entered the room and said apologetically 'Just a minute, I must see if she has him'. It may have been a story by Miss Yonge; if so, it is not unlike a reminiscence of W. E. Gladstone, who was also reading the *Heir of Redcliffe* very late when Mrs. Gladstone came to fetch him up to bed, and 'I must just see if he's confirmed', he said as an excuse.

There are many petals to add to the jar of memory, many blossoms for the gathering, but there are some flowers that shine with a strange attractive luminosity and give out a sweet fragrance at night or in the dusk. So we leave the Vicar going out in the dark of a festival morning in his first parish of Wareside, Herts, with his lantern, that he might call his flock to meet him at the altar at 5.30 a.m.

Chapter Five

HIDDEN SPRINGS

Many unseen rivulets find their way through the downs out into the valleys below, there to fill wells or to swell the main brooks. These are typical of the unseen spiritual ministries to individual souls revealed now in the Vicar's diary, now in the memories of his friends. In all Tractarian writings we are conscious of an overwhelming sense of the Holiness of God and of the sin of man; so too in the parochial diary written only for his own private use we discover a great yearning for the salvation of souls and a deep awe and reverence for Almighty God, in the light of which our present day ministries appear all too superficial. He had impressed the younger clergy with his patience and discretion, and these gifts were used to the full in his individual work, especially when dealing with the different stages of the spiritual life of one or other of his parishioners. This is specially marked by his work of conversion, bringing men and women to know themselves and to face and acknowledge their sins and whenever possible to the honesty of confession. His diary notes are instinct with his conviction that renewal must not be hurried, that it must be a movement from within, and not be imposed from without or by any insistence on rule and regulation which people were not as yet ready to accept. This was his typical English outlook—touched it may be, with compromise but making steadily for truth and honesty on the one side and for patience and pastoral care on the other.

In 1849 he notes with joy that for a whole year the Blessed Sacrament has been celebrated on all occasions

with communicants, but he adds, 'We have, however, not
worked up any yet to receive the blessed Sacrament
frequently. Indeed it is a point on which I propose to
move very gently. So long as confession is not used it is
impossible to urge very frequent Communion except for
those who by their great holiness show particular fitness.
With confession one might urge it generally.' Again, 'I
recommended Mrs. B. to come fortnightly to the blessed
Sacrament and to come to me beforehand. She thankfully
acceded.' To another he spoke of confession before a more
frequent Communion, 'She seemed eagerly to agree to
my view.' He has a 'natural fear that people who are not
"strong" should fall and not go through a deep process of
penitence from easiness, forgetfulness or the like'.

As early as 1848, the three days before Christmas, Lent,
Easter and Whitsunday, were employed in receiving
confessions in the morning and preparing communicants
in the evening. There are some notes relating to the confessions of men in 1850, and he also speaks of the difficulty
of establishing a right relationship between the priest and
his flock in spiritual matters for lack of habitual confession. 'Real opening of the heart or even consultation on
personal religion seems very far off. Neither does any
method suggest itself to me for bringing about this, the
only right subject of communication between a Priest and
his flock. A long way short of confession there might be
something of the kind, general advising, etc., but *this* men
do not seem to regard, or rather they seem to dislike. . .
How without this confidence one is to bring one's people
to an improved state, I confess I cannot see.'

Again the same note is sounded in other entries: 'I am
convinced that to raise the parish collectively, the only
method is to work upon these people individually, I mean
it cannot be effected by sermons and mass affairs. But
then how is one to get at them? They all, as far as I am

concerned, are "saints", that is they will neither confess nor allow me to find out or ask about the least fault. So that I have no chance. This is the case from the highest to the least, it is all but universal. . . . The tradesmen are still sadly slack, themselves, wives and children. They seem to think that whatever has been done ought always to be continued and merely satisfy their "conscience" by doing as few acts of religion as possible. Of course this arises from want of love, we must try and give them a desire for and a delight in religion and then all will follow. But how can we do this? The pewed Church is very much against us. We cannot work out "the beauty of holiness". Still by God's grace we are enabled to gather one or two from various quarters. We cannot convert the masses and we must be satisfied with this progress.'

Two reminiscences of those whom he directed prove that though his ideal was so high his evangelistic love always sought to make the road easy and comprehensible. One records that 'when we made our confessions at St. Michael's, the moment we opened the door the Vicar would begin with the De Profundis and we would see him with his face to the altar. It all seemed very solemn. Before I began my first confession he said to me, "Now child, remember that what you have to say cannot possibly be as bad as what I had to say." When it was over he said "Now we will just nail each of these sins to our Lord's Cross".' The other remembers the simple counsel he gave in regard to recurrent temptations: 'Why don't you just make the sign of the Cross and say to yourself "you goose"?'

Although the Vicar was so greatly troubled by the lack of spiritual communication with his people, the response seems to have been actually very rapid; we seldom realise that though Dunkirk represents a turning point in the war, it never looks like it at the time. On the Feast of

the Circumcision 1850, for instance, he found seventy-five
communicants at a Mass at a quarter before 5 a.m., and
in 1849 he writes that there was 'a better tone among the
young people than in 1847. They seem more serious,
better instructed. I have about a hundred for Confirmation, men and lads of two sorts, girls of two sorts, and
tradesmens daughters', and he records that his communicants 'talk simply and bluntly but very pleasingly, I
think', about religion.

His own grave reverent attitude towards God and holy
things must have contributed immeasurably to the gradual
awakening. A Sacristan Sister wrote of the Founder: 'I
always see (I can never forget) the awe and reverence with
which he approached the Altar; how he stood at a High
Mass during the singing of the Gospel facing north, with
tightly clasped hands, reverent and intent. The saints had
visions when they celebrated and our Founder once said
to a novice who complained that her realisation of Our
Lord's presence was very inadequate, "I never stand at
the Altar without seeing the Heavens opened." So great
was his veneration for the Holy Scriptures that when he
read the lessons he would unclasp and clasp the Bible with
extreme care. I can see him now teaching a novice how
to handle the Bible. They stood together at the lectern,
the old man and the girl. Once when he had broken his
arm the Sacristan Novice had to be at his side to turn the
pages.' He would never allow any other book to be put
on the Bible and had expressed a wish that the Bible he
had always used, a small one with small print and yellow
with age, should be buried with him. There is a contemporary account of Bishop Butler, his great namesake,
who was wrapt in awe when celebrating the Holy
Mysteries, when 'his thin face was illuminated with
divine sweetness and beauty'; there is a marked affinity
between the two men.

After the first years of his ministry in Wantage we begin to see a deepening of spiritual life recorded in the diary. In 1849 he had written of a sick person in well-to-do circumstances, belonging to a class in which it is often found difficult to speak of spiritual things. He had 'been much struck by her gentleness and calmness' after severe pain, and he continues, 'I had spoken to her of the need of self-examination and preparation for that death to which she quietly and faithfully looks. She quite understood me and said she had done what she could. I have not spoken of Absolution, but I watch my time. Yet surely so pure a spirit can hardly have committed mortal sin and confession cannot therefore be needful.' In 1850 another invalid of whom he writes is able to go further: 'She spoke most touchingly of the great blessing it had been to her that she had been converted from Methodism to the Church. Such gentleness and peace and humility as hers do more towards impressing the truth of the position of the Church on one's mind than many arguments.' And of another, 'She was gentle to the last, deeply resting on religious consolations, most thankful for my advice and prayers, fortnightly receiving the Holy Communion of Christ's Body and Blood.' After writing of the death of a parishioner, he says: 'This is one of the clearest cases of the advantage of ministerial attention. When I first went to see him, some weeks ago, he, being evidently a proud man, said rather coldly at first, when I asked him if he wished me to visit him, that he could read the Bible himself. I did not expostulate, but before I left him, he asked me spontaneously, evidently however with a struggle, to continue my visits. I therefore did, and thankfully, after a time, found his mind gradually softening. He had been, I fear, a drinking, ill-tempered knave, this in a great degree, though not technically, he confessed and showed deep penitence and thankfulness, and whenever I went

to see him, I chiefly enlarged on God's great mercy for th
truly penitent, taking as texts such passages as Our Lord'
miracles, the raising of the widow's son, etc. I also spok
from time to time to him of the Blessed Sacrament, thoug
with doubt as to the probability of his receiving it. This
however, he did. He died without a struggle of any kind
breathing his last as just before.'

Six months later we read of 'a rough fellow, once
teetotaller, who broke his pledge and until a year ag
never came to church. If I am not much mistaken, thi
man is quite changed. He never misses church, pray
regularly, never goes into a public house'. One evening
the man, being a communicant, called to see the Vicar
He had fallen into drunkenness, but once only; 'The nigh
on which he fell was a club night and he had even the
gone twice home and would have remained had his wif
been there. She had gone to look for him. He returned t
the public house and remained. He thoroughly owns hi
sin and spoke very well about it. This man has never bee
assisted by me in any way.'

Butler never fixes the blame on the laity, howeve
much he may feel that they have failed to meet him o
spiritual ground. His heart searchings probe deeply int
the single-hearted zeal of the clergy. If he laments tha
at Christmas many of the people are 'employed, I fear, i
the eating and drinking part more than in the real festivit
of the day. . . . It will be well next year', he remind
himself, 'to represent that a holy life is compatible wit
our social duties,' he has pertinent questions to ask himse
and the clergy. 'We do not sufficiently take pains to cal
on the poor and others before these great and solemn day
and explain their use and meaning. Sermons are com
paratively useless. Nothing really answers but persona
(house to house) visiting and direct addresses. This almos
always answers, and if we had all gone round to ou

people in the end of the previous week and on Monday and Tuesday, I believe the Church would have been full.' 'What is our idea of a perfect Christian?' he asks in the diary. 'I mean supposing any person submits himself or herself to our guidance what are we going to do with that person? Have we got any definite idea of where we want to take him? Or, rather like bad fencers who, even though their adversary drop his foil would not touch him because they do not thrust far enough and because they have, in fact, no idea of wounding him, so are we altogether ignorant of the road by which to guide to sanctity.'

'What are our chief faults', he asks again, 'as ministers and stewards of God's mysteries, servants to give the household their meat in due season, under-shepherds preparing for the Chief Shepherd's coming, preachers of the Gospel of Peace? Of course this book is not the place to speak of our inward faults, lack of prayers, recollection, meditation, etc. This must each know and struggle against himself. But it may be as well to mention:

'1. A lack of punctuality. This seems a subtle form of self-indulgence. Often we are driven for time, just when the service begins or the like, which we might easily have saved in the day by a little more vigorous resolution. This want of punctuality gives an unsettled character to the service, all parts of which ought to be conducted with machine-like precision. Midday prayer ought to be, so to say, sacrosanct. All else (speaking somewhat generally) ought to bend to it. It is the hinge of all our parish work.

'2. Do we weigh with sufficient care the comparative importance of the various acts we are called to perform? Occasionally of course they will clash, and are we not apt to give a preference to sight over Faith, to our own actions over the power exerted by Prayer; which is the action of God?

'3. Are we sufficiently "instant in season and out of season", ready to put aside our own arrangements to do the work of Christ?

'4. Do we not need more united prayer, both private and public, and ought we not from time to time to keep a solemn fast together for the sins of ourselves and of our people?

'5. Are we attentive enough to the cases of lingering sickness and recovery? Often more work may be done during the process of recovery than in the hour of danger, but with more difficulty, doubtless.'

In the Community notes, carefully kept, of the Founder's addresses at professions and clothings, we can penetrate more deeply into the inner garden of fruits and spices 'laid up for the Beloved'.[1]

He loved to play with the continuity of history, to trace the dedicated life from its earliest inception 'in the annals of the early church: Agnes, Thecla, Margaret, Prisca', 'old men and maidens, young men and children forsaking the world, giving themselves freely even unto death, that they might abide faithful to the perfect life, the life separated from the world and devoted to Him.' History is but a prelude for thanksgiving for the 'wonderful Providence which it has pleased God to rekindle, this spirit in this branch of Christ's Church to which we belong, after the lapse of so many years. There is the same desire to live very near to Jesus, there is the same absolute readiness to relinquish money, comfort, society: the same readiness to obey, the same desire for a virgin life; the same craving for service, for constant communion with Him, the same longing to make sacrifice for His Dear

[1] Bishop Ken gave the title of *The Spouse's Garden* to his long poem on the Virgin Life composed during the time of his residence at Naish Court, Somerset. 'The garden enclosed' is an age-old symbol of self-dedication.

Sake'. As he goes on writing, he appears to fall into meditation as if testing his words by his own life: 'If I accept this call I must reserve nothing. He will not accept a divided service. I am not *obliged* to accept, though it is surely dangerous to refuse it. But when once accepted He will have nothing less than my whole heart. "While it remained was it not mine own—after it was sold it was in mine own power" (Acts v, chapter iv). But when once I have offered it, that is to say myself, to keep back any portion, not to give Him all is that kind of hypocrisy which St. Peter calls "lying against the Holy Ghost".'

Still living in the world and meeting its varied and multitudinous claims, Butler had none the less given himself completely with no withholding, and his use of the personal pronoun brings his guidance of others home to himself in self-criticism and examination. That too was characteristic. Like St. Augustine in his treatise on virginity, he could not lay sufficient stress on the humility of heart which must accompany the high honour of the dedicated life. He had a wonderful insight into the corresponding obligations 'to school your own hearts to highest sanctity. Patiently and unweariedly to endure, to live a life of Prayer and of unremitting Labour'. He could direct others because he was ever most severe on himself. He frequently set before the novices at their Clothing the ideal of the Holy House of Nazareth in its simplicity, unity and faithful labour. Here, he said, they were to find Poverty, Chastity and Obedience in the form of joyousness, order and glad surrender of will, constantly commending the example of Our Lady under whose name he dedicated the Community: 'Behold, she said, the handmaid of the Lord God Who had chosen her and at once she answers to His choice. From that moment she is His entirely and without reserve. Her only hesitation is whether so great an honour could indeed be hers. "How shall this be?" But once satisfied, fame, comfort, worldly peace and prosperity are all abandoned. Well she knows that a sword shall pierce through her own soul, that her choice involves every sort of pain and cost. Yet she has made it and shall never withdraw. She has counted the cost and is willing to face all that follows. And depend upon it, dear Sisters, there was never one moment in Mary's life when she would have revoked her choice. Even in that bitter distress, beneath the very Cross when the Son of her love, her care, her honour, her worship hung in mortal agony, when she stood, a lone woman without child or husband—rely upon it, even then, the sense of her great honour and dignity still upheld her, the remembrance of that glorious choice by which God had chosen her and which she had ratified and accepted, gave her nerve and power and courage to whisper of that hour of anguish "Behold the handmaid of the Lord".'

It is not surprising that Butler had always felt a special love for Mother Harriet, the woman who had passed with him through the troubled waters, who had no faith in herself but whose faith in God enabled her to answer and to rise to His call. 'Always the same—timid, diffident yet full of simple faith', thus he spoke to the Sisters after her death. 'Some say the religious life is cramped and narrow, that the mind can only be developed by contact with this world's interests. I say from my own experience that the religious life develops all that is in the character more fully than aught else; if only, as in her case, there be Humility, Faith, Love, Simplicity, then God gives all else that is needed. . . . And that is the beginning of all distrust in self, our own ideas, our own desires, our own theories, putting instead our trust in God.' Speaking of Mother Harriet's deep humility, he said 'Never was one more humble than she. I remember that a man of some emience said to me on coming away from the house "That the humblest woman I have ever set eyes on".[1]

With the deep love of memory shared, Butler would dwell long and tenderly on his old friend who had 'trembled when it became evident that she only could take charge of the Community, little as it was in those days, suspected, looked down upon and often in difficulties; yet in her great humility she won her way, bringing, as I know perhaps better than any, all to God, making everything a matter of simple prayer, always distrustful of self but always full of deep strong faith in Him who had called her, being confident that He who had begun the good work would perform it until the day of Jesus Christ".' Words such as these reveal much of his own character, the man of ardent, determined will—a will, however, that was never directed to his own ends, who had set before himself the ideal of self-effacement and humility. Perhaps they hint at his own inner battles and of victory assured. Mother Harriet was herself a hidden spring, moving yet still, a source of healing and refreshment, and her character, so different to his, required the self-discipline of courage and faith while he, not lacking either, had had to learn patience and self-suppression; both lessons were perfectly learned. Within two weeks of his own death the Vicar wrote to the Superior of a branch house of the Community, 'I was at Wantage in the week before Christmas. I have had a busy time of it, people pity me for having so much work. They can hardly imagine how I love it and how it rejoices my heart to labour for the dear Sisters, nor how it helps myself to a high standard of Christian living and humbles me besides when I find myself called to help those who are so far superior to myself.'

[1] In 1878 she wrote to the Associates: 'Pray for us that, undismayed by our own weakness and fewness, we may altogether rest on Him Whose "Strength is made perfect in weakness".'

One who knew Butler well said 'he kept death always before him, not as a crippling dread but as a stimulus to exertion and a call to constant watchfulness', so that when it came, his daughter Mary tells us, 'It came as he ever wished it might come, in the very midst of his labours and with no sudden surprise. And he accepted the word of command from the Great Captain under whose banner he had been so long and strenuously fighting, to lay down his arms. He obeyed without a murmur.' 'It was the most beautiful dropping asleep, making us think of the hymn, "And now, Beloved Lord, thy soul resigning." Bishop King had said prayers twice at his side and he had joined his hands in prayer and was able to thank the Bishop at the end. The Bishop and others were downstairs, but I was in the room next to his and so had the blessed privilege of being with him at the end, saying the last prayers and the 23rd Psalm, and just as I reached the end of the Creed, *The life everlasting* his spirit passed away and the dear face looked like itself again, calm and sweet and peaceful. The nurse said she had seen many die, but never such a death as his, calm, collected, conscious to the end.' His last words to his wife, who was also near death, were: 'My Saviour is waiting for me with outstretched arms,' and then they parted and he gave himself up to die. He had given the doctor all his wishes about the funeral, no needless expense, no flowers except one cross, and how he was to be vested after death in cassock, surplice, hood and stole. His body was taken to St. Hugh's, in the Retro-choir of the Lincoln Cathedral, for the Requiem and was laid to rest in the cloister garth of the Minster.

It may have seemed pretentious and far-fetched to have linked the name of the Victorian priest with those of a King and Bishop of historic fame and to have claimed him as their true descendant and heir of the ages. The growth of a nation, a church and an individual must always be

ABOUT 1894

a matter of inheritance; each has a clear genealogical tree. Life is after all like a relay race in which one hands on the torch to another, and though we may pride ourselves on originality no one can escape the chain of history behind him. The genius inaugurates, the man of position can carry much into effect, consolidating and developing; the spiritual man bringing fire and inspiration, can kindle or re-kindle when the flame dies down. Theirs are the voices that call across the centuries, but the final issue will always depend on the common men or women who have to live the ordinary life and translate high ideals into their mother tongue. Without them the voices of the outstanding leaders are never heard, tradition is lost and inspiration falters. Between Alfred and FitzWaryn, Butler and Butler, the people of Wantage, as in every other town and village, have lived their lives, sometimes at a high level making for character and tradition, culture and spiritual understanding, sometimes at a low level content only when appetites were satisfied.

William John Butler found Wantage at its lowest but set himself to awaken it as surely as he roused the young students or called his communicants for their festival Mass. In this he succeeded, and he leaves us with the conviction that these things can be done, even when we shrink from effort as we would from a cold bath on awakening. The waters of Alfred's three streams may all look cold before we are fully aroused, but each in its way invites to cleansing and refreshment and renewed activity.

Alfred gives us an idea of what the waters of education might mean, waters of world traffic with all the inter-change of goods and commodities, widening our narrow ideas, carrying us out into a world and an universe. Books, interests, travel, values—all might be ours if we could only open our eyes to the riches that await us. Alfred was an educationalist because he loved his people and

F   B.W.

wished to gather them round him in understanding and response; Butler was an educationalist for the same reason, and because he loved he wanted to share all that he had, his advantages, his home, his money, and his time—only he kept none of his time for himself. He tried to make all that was possible available for all, from the better-to-do to the workhouse—and workhouses were workhouses in 1847—none should be left out. Education by itself may fail to enlarge the mind unless it is an attitude to life: it fails when it becomes a pigeon hole in which a few examination results are stored, it becomes the life blood of personality when it kindles observation and interest, self-discipline and discrimination.

This, too, can be counted as part of the legacy that Butler has left to us. The whole life for the whole man. His philosophy was founded on this outlook, which arose from his own zest in life and the purpose that he had set before himself.

It is the purpose in life that has been lacking of late years in this our new age, and we have been in danger of ending on the note of futility. Without a purpose, psychologists tell us, man is lost, and Jung, more explicit, has said further that of all the patients who come to consult him there are none in middle age whose ultimate need is not that of Religion. There was no sense of futility in Butler's life: its very violence, the pace, the overwork, the quick observation, the downrightness and hatred of humbug gave a sense of aim, purpose and determination. He was a fine Englishman of typical tradition, who disciplined impatience into patience but was never going to stand any nonsense. Again a legacy for us. But the finest character needs the deepest spring, that of Religion, and Butler found in this the source of all his energy, all his growth and of all the fruition of his plans. This, too, he leaves us, a legacy of longing that we also, from the least

to the greatest, may look to the holy mountains whence
come the rivers that make glad the City of God, and say
with thankful hearts 'All my fresh springs are in Thee'.

Father Maxwell, once Curate of Wantage and later
Superior of the Society of St. John the Evangelist, Cowley,
sums up in closing words:

. . . ' To the Church at large Dean Butler was probably
best known as the great organiser, the clear and incisive
teacher, the successful parish priest, the founder and for
many years the director of a great Religious Community,
the man of indomitable will who ever carried through the
plans he had so carefully laid, however long he might have
to wait for the fulfilment of his desires. But there are many
others, notably the Sisters and Exterior Sisters of the
Wantage Community, whose hearts still carry memories of
a very different side of his life and work, the side which
gave interior power for all those efforts that were out-
wardly so successful. Simple prayers, written during
retreats or after meditations or in response to appeals for
help by those who stood in intimate spiritual relationship
to the Dean, can still remind us of that almost frightening
singleness of purpose, of that unfailing sense of the claims
of duty, of that absolute confidence in the power of the
renewed will to answer to the Will of God, which so often
braced his penitents to put forth spiritual energies which
they hardly dreamed themselves to possess, and still
remind us, too, of that tender compassion and patient
forbearance and yearning love which at once forbade
him to let a soul slip out of his grasp, and taught him so
well how to wait and watch and encourage, as by degrees
it learned to depend, not upon himself, but upon Divine
Grace, and to walk with something of his own fidelity in
the ways of duty. Nothing of this can be more particularly
spoken about, it could only flourish in that hiddenness
and under that holy reserve which must necessarily veil

it from the general view. Those who had the blessing of knowing the Founder will recall the simplicity of that interior spirit which was the true secret hidden within that life of ceaseless activity.'

'Happy is the man who waits: to him
    comes fulfilment, holy acceptance.
It is as in spring—a gentle interplay
    of expectation and hallowed blossoming.'

JULIUS TYCIAK, *Life in Christ*.[1]

[1] By kind permission of Messrs. Sheed & Ward.

THE CONVENT 1863

HIS LEGACY

It is fifty years since William John Butler went to his rest; he had laid many foundations, digging deep with patience and determination, yet he never saw the full fruition of his toil. Looking back we may fairly discern what such a discipline must have meant to a strong-willed man; but looking round at the building that he was preparing by 'faith, grind and prayer', his daughters of St. Mary the Virgin, Wantage, are compelled to recall something of the growth and extension of the Convent on 'Limburh' in gratitude to their founder, even if it be to break for a moment through that reticence and reserve with which he endowed them.[1]

The Community was not born in times that could be called propitious, and the first twenty-five years of its life were marked by disturbance and upheaval in the outer world. The Chartist Movement was gathering strength, Paris was in the throes of the Commune, Garibaldi had opened his first unsuccessful campaign, and as the years passed, this unrest was to pass on to the Crimean War in Europe and to the war of the North and South in America. Yet in contrast to this the romantic movement still lingered in England, 'the Gothic' remained in fashion, ruins, especially by moonlight, were a supreme attraction and the lyrical and sentimental were at the height of popularity. Religion, as we have seen, was conventional in setting and outlook; wigs were still worn by the higher ecclesiastics, the three-decker remained in place, galleries,

[1] For further details see: *A Hundred Years of Blessing*, S.P.C.K.

proprietory pews, responses made by the parish clerk, charity children and almshouse women in uniform were all considered seemly and unchangeable. Social customs followed suit and class distinctions were part of an unalterable law; chaperones were indispensable and young ladies were indeed young ladies, with all the elegance of nerves and emotions, of archness and ignorance. No trend of current thought would appear to have been specially favourable to the foundation of a Community, and even if the romantic school had led in that direction it would have inclined to over-decoration, over-emphasis after the manner of the 1851 Exhibition, a papier maché version of art and history, delightful indeed to the collector of curios but contributing little else.

Even the rise of prosperity after the Napoleonic Wars, although not shared by the common people, helped only to raise another materialistic barrier against anything that approached self-immolation, while an over-conservative, over-comfortable church neither inspired nor led the way. None the less, dissatisfaction and disillusionment, the almost inevitable aftermath of war, were present and there was a perceptible awakening to the fact of sin, to duty and responsibility, to the inexcusable poverty of the masses and the urgent need for enlightened assistance. Men's eyes were gradually opening to the problems of slavery overseas as well as to the bad social conditions, not unallied to it, that obtained at home. And this ground swell, this current moving below the surface of the water had actually reached the 'young ladies', with Florence Nightingale as the first adventurous rebel and Charlotte Mary Yonge to mark a more pedestrian way; they too had begun to think.

A somewhat distracted world did not distract William John Butler, nor did the crying need for work and workers cause him to hurry; he was content to go slowly and the growth of his religious foundation followed suit, but nobody worried. Mother Harriet and Sister Charlotte, for example, had arrived in 1849 and were professed in 1850, and this certainly lost no time, but Harriet was not installed canonically as Mother until 1854. They had to wait until 1863 before being known as 'Sisters of St. Mary the Virgin', and their Community was not actually dedicated to St. Mary the Virgin until 1865, when they took as their motto 'Ecce Ancilla Domini, fiat mihi secundum verbum tuum', introducing at the same time a memorial of Our Lady into the Office to commemorate her virtues of 'lowliness, obedience and faithfulness'. It is doubtful whether Butler had known anything of the Domrahamme, or had even paid sufficient respect to the ancient Chapel of St. Mary the Virgin just outside the Parish Church, as it was pulled down during his incumbency, but wittingly or unwittingly he linked his little family to past history by their dedication.

Thus the Sisters entered their new life unlabelled and domiciled in back streets, while specifically instructed by the founder himself to be inconspicuous in their work, their dwelling and their dress. The latter must have resembled that of the Regents of Alet, the foundation of Nicholas Pavillon in the seventeenth century, of which Dom Claude Lancelot gives the following account:

'They wear dark stuffs which reach close to their throat with full sleeves down to the wrists: their handkerchiefs also come close up to the throat and their caps, which are very neat, cover the whole of their hair, excepting a little on the forehead.' It is remembered that once Butler told the Sisters to 'look as much as possible like his wife'; good ladies in those days were invariably draped in shawls, with full skirts and neat 'workhouse' bonnets.

Humility can never be exactly an exciting virtue, but when it is thus inconspicuously clothed even to identifica-

tion with the crowd it must surely have gone very deep.
It was this attitude of mind and heart and offering that
the Founder so constantly underlined, the tradition of
utter simplicity and of steadfast loyalty to the Church of
England. Growing inwardly leads to strength, and this
may be why Bishop Randall, who succeeded Butler in
the Office of Warden, was able to speak of 'the mas-
culine character of the Community'.

If the Founder worked slowly, even to the apparent
neglect of outward forms, he laid a considerable canonical
observance upon the few Sisters, by adding Matins and
Evensong to the sevenfold Office. He thus assigned a high
place to the little Society according to Roman Catholic
estimates of observance,[1] for this involved the recitation
of the whole Psalter monthly. Of late years, however, the
substance of the Night Hours, including the recitation of
the Psalms so as to complete the Day Hours and the Choir
lections of Scripture, have been transferred until after
Compline. Two hours and a half were also assigned by
the Founder from the earliest days for daily private
devotion. The rule and constitutions of the Community,
based on those of St. Augustine, were not completed until
1896, after forty years of careful and prayerful thought
and experience. His almost scrupulous testing before any
advance was made was part of the Founder's hatred of
anything unreal or sentimental and made his personal
influence strong and bracing. This revival of the religious
life therefore marked a return to the spirit of St. Ambrose,
St. Jerome and St. Augustine, and had little to do with the
elaborations of the fourteenth and fifteenth centuries.
Indeed, notwithstanding Butler's special devotion to St.
François de Sales and to French Catholicism, he did not
follow the saint in his more flowery writings, disliking, on

[1] This was the opinion of the Abbé Portal who visited the Convent
in 1894.

the other hand, the current evangelical appeal to the emotions.

It was natural that he placed his Sisters under a strict obedience to the Episcopate, and in this they had no reason for regret, as the succeeding Bishops of Oxford, from Bishop Wilberforce to the present Bishop, have upheld and guided their work at every stage. Such then were the foundations so truly laid without any sign of impatience or desire to see the increase; but since those early years the Community has been allowed to contribute to Catholic worship by imagery, printing, research and art, especially in the production of the plain chant of the Latin Breviary of 1531, adapted to English words by the skill of the Rev. G. Palmer, Mus. Doc. This has entailed the development of a printing press with carefully selected type, both for words and notation. The Sisters have made use of the method of Solesmes in Choir and this too has brought friendly ecclesiastics from the continent to study and, fortunately, to approve.

It must be apparent, however, that after the Opus Dei of prayer and worship the primary responsibility of the Community has been that of education; it could not be otherwise according to the mind of the Founder and to the whole foundation. School work is undertaken in the three main schools in England, two in India and two in Africa, with an average of nearly two hundred pupils in each, all of which schools are under Government inspection. Indeed, when the Board of Education in 1901-1902 offered to inspect unaided secondary schools, Sir Michael Sadler while speaking at a meeting in Cambridge, referred to the fact, that the Schools of St. Mary's Community were the first on the list to apply for recognition.

Finally in 1925 a house was acquired in the Banbury Road, Oxford, as a hostel for students in the university. The response was immediate and two other adjoining

houses were added subsequently to meet increasing
demands. In this hostel the Sisters of the Community
serve each generation in a spirit of understanding,
primarily by their own life of devotion in the recitation
of the Divine Office in the Chapel, thus continually
dedicating to God the intellectual energy of the university.

Another educational branch, already mentioned as
developing from the College for pupil teachers at St.
Michael's, is the Guild of the Good Shepherd for primary
and secondary teachers. This has a large and steadily
increasing membership, representing a variety of nationali-
ties in many lands: some of the members have been
sufferers or actual victims of the war. The Guild has in
turn given birth to the Third Order of Jesus the Good
Shepherd for qualified teachers and youth leaders, an
authorised religious society having its centre at West
Ogwell, Devon, a Third Order Regular with its own
novitiate. Other 'daughters' have been given to the
Community of St. Mary the Virgin, who are affiliated to
the Mother House though otherwise independent. The
Society of Servants of the Cross, founded in 1877 at
Fulham and removed to Worthing in 1882 and now at
the Convent of the Holy Rood, Findon, Worthing, has its
own novitiate and constitution. The Community of the
Holy Name at Poona for Indian women was founded in
1905 but, owing to present unrest, there are not at the
moment so many vocations, for India is passing through
its time of testing. The Community of St. John the Baptist
at St. Cuthbert's Mission, Cape Province, South Africa,
was founded in 1914 for African women, with its own
convent, novitiate and branch house, the Sisters retaining
the ordinary African standard of custom and living. The
Servants of Mary, founded in 1919, who specialize in
domestic work and the care of the aged, also have their

own Mother House, rule and novitiate. The Society of the Salutation, founded in 1942, is as yet feeling and testing its way in the religious life, but the need has arisen for those who, having vocation, have hitherto been precluded from entering existing convents on account of age or some delicacy of health. They are at present specially devoted to prayer but are free to continue art or embroidery, and other manual occupations. Like their forerunners of the Visitation in France they have been led to enclosure. Thus the founder's aspiration to include the vocation of Mary with that of Martha has been wonderfully realised.

Though education has always had the foremost place in the Sisters' active life, the Community has never given up the work of reclaiming women and girls that was laid upon it by Henry Manning before his secession to Rome. Even here Butler's thoroughness, enthusiasm and influence gave a strong educational emphasis, thus making it easy, when the time came, for the 'homes' and 'refuges' and 'houses of mercy' to become approved schools under Government. Eight branch houses are devoted to such Moral Welfare work, as well as one to Maternity work and one to the care of young children while four other houses are concerned with general mission work in parishes. The difficult conditions of war (including as they have the bombing of branch houses), have further developed another work already begun for the care of aged and elderly ladies. Five branch houses are now devoted to this, two of which include hospital wards.

The first call to work overseas came in 1877 from Bishop Mylne of Bombay to the central stronghold of Hinduism in India, Poona; in the heart of the native city Christian parochial work has been gradually built up, complete with medical service in the dispensary and hospital and with a large, well-built primary and Anglo-vernacular School for both girls and boys; embroidery and other workrooms; in fact, all the ordinary activities of a parish. This work, since its foundation, has been under the direction of the Society of St. John the Evangelist, Cowley. In Poona Camp St. Mary's European School educates a large proportion of Indian as well as English girls and in 1938 the Community undertook the direction of St. Peter's School at Khandala, an Anglo-Indian and Indian centre on the Bombay Ghats, but were obliged to relinquish it for various reasons in 1947.

In 1903 Sisters went forth to South Africa to undertake a school in Pretoria directly after the signing of the Peace of Vereeniging. Moral Welfare work was developed at Irene, near Pretoria, and has grown to large dimensions, while in the native Transkei, Cape Province, the Sisters co-operate with the Society of St. John the Evangelist in educational and mission service for the Africans, specialising in the care of S. Lucy's Hospital and in practical domestic training. The latest development has come in the present war, when the Sisters have had the privilege of continuing Miss Dorothy Maud's wonderful work in Sophiatown, Johannesburg, having the additional experience of being torpedoed on the way out! In 1946 the Community undertook the charge of S. Mary's School of over 300 girls at Waverley, a suburb of Johannesburg. The Sister Superior was the first Sister to travel to her post by air.

The Community has to record its indebtedness to the goodly company of Priests and women Associates who have given generously of their time, money and prayer. Among many familiar names in such a record there stands that of Charlotte Mary Yonge, who became an Associate in 1868 and asked to have her vocation tested. She was, however, dissuaded from this latter course, as it was thought she would exercise a wider influence by continuing to write. A further and more regularized group in connection with the Mother House is rapidly increasing, that of the Third Order of St. Mary the Virgin, women who, while still living in the world, desire to keep a strict rule of life. As many of its members are in the National Services at the present time the Community may claim that it is offering of its best to the country and is bringing a strong quiet influence to bear on young life.

The Founder wrote to the Associates in 1887:

'Such then is the record of the tale we have to tell. To those of us who remember the small beginnings in the little house in Newbury Street, Wantage, it is indeed surprising to see to what it has grown. We can only exclaim, "It is the Lord's doing and it is marvellous in our eyes." No one except those who have been intimately connected with us can know the effort and the anxiety which all this has cost and costs. We have, it may be, undertaken more than our weak strength can altogether justify. It is however hard to be prudent when the demand comes to help living souls. If we have transgressed in this way, we trust that the great call and need for Sisters' services may plead as our excuse. For it is universally found that in no other way than this can be secured continuity of work, discipline, and skill which is the result of experience, and therefore it is that they who are engaged in the great conflict between good and evil are ever urgent for such help as religious communities can give, and it is hard indeed to refuse.

'Our Sisters live as plainly as is compatible with health. Our buildings are unornamented save by good proportions and good arrangement. The only decorations of our Chapels are music and cared for services which cost only labour and time.'

The two small loaves laid upon the Altar in 1850 have

indeed been blessed and multiplied. The founder never saw the fulness of growth, but he was blessed because he did not see and yet believed. He worked with slow patience, but the Lord said 'The little one shall become a thousand and the small one a strong nation. I, the Lord, will hasten the time.'

A.M.D.G.

m
3/50

Domrahamme

DCCCXlVIIJ

ROME
GAUL
BRITAIN

THE HAM.